TABLE OF CONTENTS

CHAPTER 3: MASTERING COMPOSITION AND FRAMING

The Rule of Thirds and Beyond: Creative Framing Techniques

Using Depth and Perspective in Your Shots

How to Find the Best Angles for Stunning Photos

CHAPTER 4: LIGHTING TECHNIQUES FOR IPHONE PHOTOGRAPHY

Understanding Natural vs. Artificial Light

How to Use the iPhone's Night Mode for Low-Light Photography

Controlling Exposure and Using HDR

CHAPTER 5: ADVANCED PHOTOGRAPHY TECHNIQUES

Mastering ProRAW: When and How to Use It

Capturing Motion: Action Shots and Burst Mode

INTRODUCTION TO IPHONE 15 PRO PHOTOGRAPHY

With mobile photography changing the game in recent years, the iPhone 15 Pro has become a revolutionary tool for both professional and amateur photographers to record and share memories. The days of needing a specialized camera to take excellent pictures and movies are long gone. With the iPhone 15 Pro, you can effortlessly produce breathtaking graphics thanks to its powerful imaging technology, expanded computational photography capabilities, and configurable camera arrangement. The device puts the world of photography right at your fingertips.

With the iPhone 15 Pro, hardware and software advances are seamlessly combined to improve your photographic experience. With its mix of ultra-wide, wide, and telephoto lenses, A17 Bionic CPU from Apple, and next-generation picture signal processing, this gadget goes beyond what is thought to be feasible from a smartphone camera. With the ability to capture both precise close-ups and beautiful vistas, the iPhone 15 Pro is a powerful tool that will satisfy the demands of any photography lover.

The goal of this book is to help you become an expert iPhone 15 Pro photographer. Whether you're a beginner or an experienced photographer seeking to improve, this book will guide you through the key features, tools, and strategies that make the iPhone 15 Pro the best camera partner. This in-depth tutorial will enable you to realize your full creative potential by teaching you everything from how to use sophisticated tools for picture editing to comprehending the technical components of the camera system. In the pages that follow, you'll delve into the principles of mobile photography, examine useful advice for taking beautiful pictures in various settings, and learn editing methods that will elevate your photos above the ordinary. With the iPhone 15 Pro, you can capture ordinary events or take on artistic photography projects with more accuracy and elegance in your narrative telling.

Join us as we explore the many opportunities presented by iPhone 15 Pro photography, where there is always a chance to produce something really amazing.

CHAPTER 1

WHY THE IPHONE 15 PRO IS A GAME-CHANGER FOR PHOTOGRAPHY

Because of its strong mix of cutting-edge technology and smart software, the iPhone 15 Pro is a game-changer for photography, making it easy for both novice and expert photographers to take breathtaking photographs. The iPhone 15 Pro is a milestone in mobile photography thanks to a number of noteworthy features:

1. Sophisticated Camera Configuration

The triple-lens camera system of the iPhone 15 Pro has been improved with notable gains in sensor size, picture processing, and optical zoom capabilities. Even in difficult lighting settings, the main wide lens's bigger sensor enables for improved light collection, producing clearer and more detailed photographs. With the increased framing freedom offered by the ultra-wide lens, users may take group photos or expansive landscapes with remarkable clarity. In the meanwhile, the telephoto lens provides an optical zoom of up to 6x, enabling close-ups that are detailed without compromising the quality of the picture.

2. Digital Image processing

the iPhone 15 Pro's combination of powerful computational photography is one of its most innovative features. The phone uses machine learning algorithms, powered by the A17 Pro CPU, to improve each and every picture. Even in low light conditions, features like Smart HDR 5, Deep Fusion, and Night Mode ensure correct colors, balanced contrast, and amazing detail by combining numerous exposures and processing photos in real-time.

3. Capabilities for ProRAW and ProRes

The ProRAW and ProRes file formats on the iPhone 15 Pro make it a flexible tool for pros and hobbyists alike. With ProRAW, you can take raw photos and have total control over post-production adjustments like white balance, exposure, and noise reduction. Similarly, ProRes video recording gives users the ability to record cinema-quality video straight to their device, giving them a great deal of versatility when it comes to editing and color grading.

4. Advanced Video Capturing

The video capabilities of the iPhone 15 Pro are also quite amazing. It can capture very smooth video by shooting in 4K at 60 frames per second with improved stabilization. It also includes Cinematic Mode, which enables producers to create films with professional-caliber focus transitions and depth control. The iPhone 15 Pro improves the quality of your video footage whether you're recording intimate moments or producing material for work-related initiatives.

5. AI-Powered Improvements

Apple's persistent emphasis on artificial intelligence has yielded features like as enhanced bokeh effects and Portrait Lighting, which elevate portrait photography to a professional level. Acquiring accurate photographs of moving objects is facilitated by AI-powered depth mapping and focus tracking, which is perfect for action photography and wildlife photography.

6. Superior Display Quality

Another important feature that makes taking pictures easier is the Super Retina XDR display on the iPhone 15 Pro. With deeper blacks and brighter highlights, images and videos will seem vivid and realistic thanks to its high-resolution, high-contrast screen. Photographers don't need a separate device to evaluate, edit, and share their work because of the accuracy of the display on their phone.

7. Accessibility and Simplicity

The iPhone 15 Pro's ability to strike a mix between high-end photographic features and approachable design is what really sets it apart from the competition. The camera app's advanced functions are smoothly integrated, making it simple for anybody to use the Pro-level capabilities without requiring a significant learning curve. Regardless of experience level, the iPhone 15 Pro enables users to capture amazing images and movies with little to no effort.

KEY CAMERA FEATURES AND WHAT THEY MEAN FOR YOUR PHOTOS

The camera on the iPhone 15 Pro is brimming with capabilities that will take your shooting to new levels. These cutting-edge tools are more than just technical speak; they have practical uses that will make it easier for you to take beautiful, high-quality pictures. Let's explore some of the most important camera settings and how they affect your images.

1. A primary 48 MP sensor with quad-pixel technology

the iPhone 15 Pro's 48-megapixel primary sensor, which makes use of Quad-Pixel technology, is one of its most notable features. This implies that the camera may combine four pixels into one to improve the quality of the picture, particularly in dim light. It ensures sharpness and clarity in all lighting conditions by reducing noise in nighttime photographs and enabling you to take incredibly detailed photos during the day.

What it means for your photos: The 48MP sensor produces detailed, high-resolution photographs that are perfect for shooting close-ups, portraits, or landscapes. While daytime images are clear and rich in color, nighttime photographs become more colorful and distinct.

2. 4K HDR Cinematic Mode

you may produce films with a narrow depth of focus using the Cinematic Mode, which is close to the look of professional filmmaking. This feature, which is now available in 4K HDR, offers even more resolution and contrast, giving your films a polished and gorgeous appearance.

What that implies for your pictures: Despite being a video tool, Cinematic Mode may assist you in honing your still-photo composition skills. Similar to portrait photography, you may use background blur to highlight your subject and improve the narrative quality of your pictures.

3. RAW and High-Def

With support for ProRAW for images and ProRes for films, the iPhone 15 Pro gives you expert-level control over your material. ProRAW allows you to edit with more freedom while maintaining the whole dynamic range and level of detail in your photos. ProRes guarantees that your movies are recorded in high definition, which facilitates post-production editing.

What that implies for your pictures: With ProRAW, you can edit images in more depth by adjusting exposure, color, and tone without sacrificing picture quality. You can use your iPhone to take images that are worthy of a magazine since you can adjust them to your precise preference.

4. 6x Optical Zoom Telephoto Lens

With the iPhone 15 Pro's telephoto lens, you can get up close to your subject without sacrificing picture quality thanks to its up to 6x optical zoom. In contrast to digital zoom, which just enlarges the pixels and often results in a loss of clarity, optical zoom employs the lens to magnify the picture. What that means for your photos: The 6x optical zoom guarantees that you can catch your subject clearly, without sacrificing clarity or quality, whether you're photographing animals, a concert, or any other event from a distance.

5. The Photonic Engine

Apple's most recent advancement in computational photography is the Photonic Engine, which enhances the camera's performance in difficult lighting situations. This feature improves texture, color, and detail in all of your photos—especially those taken in dimly lit areas—by using cutting-edge machine learning and artificial intelligence.

What that implies for your pictures: The Photonic Engine makes sure that your photos maintain their depth and richness even when you shoot in low light. Better color reproduction and detail will be seen in all types of photos, including poorly lit interiors and nighttime portraiture.

6. Close-up Photography

With the enhanced macro photography option on the iPhone 15 Pro, you can take remarkably detailed close-up photos. This is ideal for taking pictures of tiny things, such as flowers, insects, or complex items, since it can capture minute details that are often unseen to the unaided eye.

What it implies for your photos: You may use macro photography to produce visually striking, even dreamlike images of commonplace items. For photos of jewelry, wildlife, or any subject where minute details count for a lot, the close-up clarity is perfect.

7. Enhanced Night Mode

The iPhone 15 Pro's Night Mode has been improved to provide quicker and more precise low-light picture taking. When you choose Night Mode, the camera knows it and automatically adjusts exposure to make sure your pictures are clear, sharp, and noise-free.

What this implies for your photos: You can

take more pictures in low light situations, such as indoor gatherings, city streets at night, or sunsets, when you use Night Mode. You won't need a flash or any other lighting equipment to get crisp, well-lit nighttime photos.

8. In-Deep Fusion

In situations with moderate to low light, Deep Fusion technology optimizes texture, detail, and noise via sophisticated machine learning. The camera takes many pictures at various exposures, then combines the best elements of each picture to produce a single, excellent picture.

What this implies for your images: Deep Fusion works particularly well for photos with a lot of texture, skin tones, and portraiture. Even in challenging lighting conditions, your photos will have a balanced appearance with natural tones and more realistic surfaces.

9. Smart HDR 5: This tool evens out your image's brightest and darkest areas. In order to bring out detail in both shadows and

highlights and ensure that no area of your picture is overexposed or underexposed, it takes numerous exposures and combines them.

What that implies for your pictures: High contrast situations, such as a bright sky over a gloomy countryside, are ideal for Smart HDR 5. It guarantees that every aspect of the picture is appropriately exposed and illuminated, producing balanced, vibrant images.

THE POWER OF COMPUTATIONAL PHOTOGRAPHY

The way we take and edit photos has been completely transformed by computational photography, especially with devices like the iPhone 15 Pro. In contrast to conventional photography, which only makes use of the physical characteristics of lenses and sensors, computational photography makes use of sophisticated algorithms and machine learning to provide previously unattainable picture enhancements.

Computational photography relies on the powerful computing capability of current devices to do tasks like instantaneous detail refinement, exposure adjustment, and picture fusion. For example, the iPhone 15 Pro's camera captures more than one picture when you take a picture. Rather, it quickly takes a number of pictures, then use algorithms to combine the best elements of each frame into a single, high-quality picture.

Without requiring a lot of manual editing, this method helps to sharpen details, enhance dynamic range, and minimize noise, resulting in results that are professional-grade.

The capacity of computational photography to function in low light is one of its biggest advantages. This technology is used by features like Night Mode to retain color fidelity, brighten photos, and show details even in difficult lighting situations. It greatly increases the accessibility and efficacy of handheld photography at night or in poorly light environments.

There's also the benefit of portrait photography. Computational photography can apply complex bokeh effects, simulate various lighting situations, and separate the subject from the backdrop using its powerful depth detection and AI-based analysis. This changes the quality of portraiture taken with smartphones, making it more akin to that of DSLR cameras.

Furthermore, computational photography is

essential to the recording of videos because it makes features like real-time HDR, automated stabilization, and improved focus possible. Thanks to these developments, consumers may now record cinema-quality footage straight from their phones.

CHAPTER 2

GETTING STARTED WITH THE IPHONE 15 PRO CAMERA

OVERVIEW OF THE IPHONE 15 PRO'S CAMERA APP

The Camera app on the iPhone 15 Pro is intended to improve both amateur and professional photography by combining cutting-edge features with basic design. One of the most advanced camera systems available today is found in the iPhone 15 Pro thanks to Apple. It boasts a triple-lens arrangement with a wide, ultra-wide, and telephoto lens, a bigger sensor, and enhanced image processing capabilities. Important characteristics:

1. Redesigned Interface: The iPhone 15 Pro's Camera app has a clear, user-friendly interface with simplified controls that make it

simple to use for both novice and expert photographers. The primary screen provides easy access to basic features like lens switching and exposure adjustment, while more sophisticated settings are discreetly hidden for photographers who want to focus on fine-tuning their photos.

2. Improved ProRAW and ProRes Capabilities: With Apple's continued development of both formats, users may now shoot in high-resolution, editable RAW files for still images and ProRes for motion pictures. Professionals who want more control over post-production will find this feature especially useful since it enables high dynamic range (HDR) editing and more freedom in color grading.

3. Cinematic Mode: The iPhone 15 Pro has an improved version of the Cinematic Mode, which was first available with the iPhone 13. This tool automatically switches focus between subjects to produce breathtaking cinematic sequences in your films, giving them professional-grade depth-of-field

effects. It now allows for 4K recording at greater frame rates and provides further control over depth of field and focus transitions.

4. Improvements to Night Mode: Apple's sophisticated machine learning algorithms, paired with the larger sensor, allow for better light capture, reduced noise, and enhanced details, making it easier to take sharp photos in difficult lighting conditions. Night Mode has been further optimized for the iPhone 15 Pro, improving its ability to capture clear and bright images in low-light environments.

5. Photographic Styles: The iPhone 15 Pro has enhanced Photographic Styles that let users customize the warmth and tone of their images. You have the option to create your own style or choose from established options like Rich Contrast, Vibrant, Warm, or Cool. Different from basic filters, these styles are cleverly integrated into the image processing pipeline, allowing you to alter certain areas of the picture while maintaining important

features and skin tones.

6. Improvements to the Portrait Mode: The iPhone 15 Pro's Portrait Mode now offers more control over depth and more realistic bokeh effects. In order to give customers more creative freedom, Apple has now included the option to change the degree of background blur after the shot is taken. This is especially helpful for taking sharply focused, natural-looking photographs with professional-grade lighting.

7. Action Mode: Enhanced video stabilization is provided via Action Mode, which was first available on the iPhone 15 Pro. With the aid of this setting, users may record video with fewer tremors even while capturing dynamic events like sports or persons moving quickly. For those who want to record exciting occasions without sacrificing the quality of their videos, this is ideal.

8. Macro Photography: The iPhone 15 Pro's ultra-wide lens makes macro photography possible, enabling users to take close-up

pictures of tiny things in order to capture their fine features. The improved focusing technology makes sure that photos stay clear and colorful even when they are just a few centimeters away.

Easy to Use: The Camera app is still easy to use even with its extensive list of professional functions. A single swipe may be used to transition between several camera modes, including picture, video, portrait, and slo-mo. Additionally, the iPhone 15 Pro adds extra on-screen guidelines to aid customers in precisely framing their photos.

AI-Powered Image Processing: The iPhone 15 Pro's sophisticated computational photography is powered by Apple's A17 Bionic technology, which guarantees that every picture and video is optimized for sharpness, detail, and dynamic range. Intelligent HDR intelligently blends many exposures to produce well-balanced photos, and machine learning algorithms improve

texture and color accuracy without human
intervention.

UNDERSTANDING CAMERA SETTINGS AND MODES

With its many advanced features and settings, the iPhone 15 Pro camera lets you take amazing pictures and films in a variety of scenarios. However, it's crucial to comprehend the primary camera settings and modes accessible to you in order to completely realize its potential. The essential knowledge to maximize the capabilities of your iPhone 15 Pro camera is outlined here.

1. Capture Mode

This is the best setting for regular shooting and is the default preset in the Camera app. using a combination of hardware and software, computational photography is used by the iPhone 15 Pro to produce high-quality photographs. When you use the camera in Photo Mode, exposure, focus, and lighting are automatically adjusted by the camera to produce sharp, detailed photographs.

• Smart HDR: Maintains clarity in both bright

and dark regions while automatically enhancing dynamic range by combining several exposures into a single photo.

• Deep Fusion: Using cutting-edge machine learning, this feature highlights textures and details when turned on in medium to low light.

• ProRAW: With this option, you can take RAW photos, which preserve more picture data than JPEG or HEIF files and provide you more editing freedom.

2. Mode of Portrait

By subtly blurring the backdrop and enhancing the depth-of-field effect (bokeh) in your images, Portrait Mode helps your subjects stand out. You have greater creative freedom with the iPhone 15 Pro since you can modify the focal point and the amount of background blur (aperture) after the photo is taken.

• Lighting Effects: To improve your photographs, choose from a range of studio-caliber lighting effects, such as Natural Light,

Studio Light, and Stage Light.

• Depth Control: For a more customized appearance, use a simple slider to change the degree of background blur.

3. Dim Lighting

when taking photos in low light or at night, the iPhone 15 Pro automatically enters Night Mode. This option enhances the brightness of your images and highlights details in low light conditions. It operates by combining many exposures taken over a short period of time into a single, brightly lighted picture.

• Manual Control: You may manually change the exposure for longer images to brighten gloomy situations, even though the camera normally does this automatically.

• Tripod Support: By using a tripod, you can take better, motion-free nighttime photographs with extended exposure durations.

4. The Cinematic Style

The Cinematic Mode is intended for storytelling-focused video recording. It enhances your movies with depth-of-field effects by automatically adjusting focus between subjects to replicate the appearance of high-end film cameras.

• Focus Transitions: Adding dynamic elements to your films, the camera can cleverly change focus between subjects as they move into or out of frame.

• Manual Focus Control: You can also use tapping to manually adjust focus, which enables you to lock focus on a specific topic or make sharp focus adjustments.

• 4K HDR Recording: For crisp, colorful films, Cinematic Mode allows for recording in breathtaking 4K HDR quality.

5. Mode of Action

When you're moving or shooting fast-paced scenarios, Action Mode is ideal for capturing steady, smooth footage. It makes use of cutting-edge stabilization technology to minimize shakiness and provide fluid, cinematic video—even while shooting handheld or while moving.

• Automatic Stabilization: Real-time adjustments to the stabilization are made by the iPhone's powerful A17 CPU and integrated sensors, which provide smooth and stable video.

• Wide-Angle Compatibility: The ultra-wide lens of the iPhone allows you to capture action-packed moments from a wider angle without compromising on quality.

6. Manual Mode, or Pro Mode

The Pro Mode, which can be accessed via third-party applications or as an inbuilt function of the camera, gives photography lovers complete control over their settings by allowing manual modification of important parameters like ISO, shutter speed, white balance, and focus.

• ISO: Regulates how sensitive the camera is to light. In bright settings, a lower ISO works best; in low light, a higher ISO works better.

• Shutter Speed: You may manage the duration of the camera's light exposure by adjusting the shutter speed. While slower speeds may provide motion blur for aesthetic impact, faster speeds freeze motion.

• White Balance: Modifies the color temperature to make sure your photos seem realistic in a variety of lighting scenarios.

7. Using Panorama Mode

Using Panorama Mode, you may take lengthy, expansive shots of the outdoors by combining many photographs into one. All you have to do is gently move your camera in one direction, and the iPhone will stitch the frames together to create a panoramic picture with excellent clarity.

• Alignment Control: As you pan around the scene, the iPhone assists you in maintaining the steadiness and alignment of your camera, resulting in a fluid, reliable output.

• Horizontal and Vertical Panoramas: These may be taken of towering buildings or landscapes; however they are usually taken horizontally.

8. Extended Mode

you may capture very detailed close-up

photos using Macro Mode. It's ideal for catching the minute details of little items like textures, flowers, or insects.

• Automatic Switching: As you approach your subject, the camera automatically shifts to the ultra-wide lens, enabling you to concentrate on minute details at as little as 2 cm away.

• Enhanced Detail: When used in conjunction with Deep Fusion, Macro Mode brings out textures and patterns in your subject that are invisible to the unaided eye.

HOW TO CHOOSE THE BEST CAMERA LENSES (WIDE, ULTRA-WIDE, TELEPHOTO)

Choosing the appropriate lens for your camera may have a big influence on the look and feel of your photos. For example, the iPhone 15 Pro has three lenses: Telephoto, Wide, and Ultra-Wide, each of which is appropriate for a certain kind of photography. You will get the finest outcomes if you are aware of their advantages and optimal usage scenarios.

1. Broad Lens

Both conventional cameras and smartphones often come with a wide lens by default. With a 24mm focal length, the wide lens on the iPhone 15 Pro is quite versatile and perfect for a range of situations.

• When to Use a Wide-Angle Lens:

o Everyday Capturing: Because it closely resembles what the human eye perceives, it's ideal for recording everyday occurrences.

o Landscapes and Cityscapes: It is ideal for outdoor photography because to its broad field of vision, which aids in capturing vast sceneries.

o Group Shots: A wide lens makes sure that everyone fits in the frame without distortion while you're snapping pictures of a group of people.

• Advantages: o Well-balanced field of vision.

o Ideal for settings with little light.

o Perfect for a variety of uses, including landscapes and portraiture.

2. Extremely Broad Lens

The iPhone 15 Pro's ultra-wide lens, which has a focal length of around 13mm, offers an even wider viewpoint. It's especially helpful for images that are dramatic or artistic since it captures more of the scene in the frame and covers a greater area.

When Is the Ultra-Wide Lens Useful?

o Architectural Photography: The ultra-wide lens makes sure the whole structure fits into your photo whether you're taking pictures of enormous structures or interiors with elaborate decorations.

o Action Shots: An ultra-wide lens helps capture more of the scene while taking pictures of subjects that are moving quickly, like athletes.

o Creative Perspectives: It may provide unusual perspectives and distortions that give your pictures flare and enhance the immersion of the situation.

• Advantages: o Exceptionally broad field of vision for views that are vast.

o Excellent at cramming big things into the frame.

o Perfect for close-ups without sacrificing backdrop or context.

3. The Telephoto Lens

On devices like the iPhone 15 Pro, the telephoto lens has a larger focal length, often between 48mm and 120mm. This lens, which has optical zoom capabilities, is excellent in enlarging in on far-off objects without compromising picture quality.

• How to Use a Telephoto Lens When?

o Self-portraiture: With its small depth of focus and ability to compress the backdrop, the telephoto lens is a great choice for portrait photography.

o Wildlife Photography: The telephoto lens allows you to zoom in while preserving clear details when you can't get near to your subject, like in wildlife photography.

o Isolated Details: Use this lens to draw attention to minute details, such face expressions or architectural features, while obfuscating background distractions.

• Advantages: o Good at zooming without sacrificing quality.

o Perfect for close-ups and portraits.

o Uses a small depth of focus to create stunning bokeh effects.

CHAPTER 3

MASTERING COMPOSITION AND FRAMING

THE RULE OF THIRDS AND BEYOND: CREATIVE FRAMING TECHNIQUES

In photography, one of the most important rules is the Rule of Thirds. By dividing the frame into nine equal pieces using two horizontal and two vertical lines, it aids photographers in producing balanced and aesthetically pleasing photos. Instead of just centering the subject, the goal is to arrange important compositional components along these lines or at their intersections to produce more dynamic and intriguing images. A more captivating shot is produced when the primary subject is positioned off-center since the viewer's attention is naturally pulled to these intersections.

Using the iPhone 15 Pro to Apply the Rule of Thirds

the grid function in the camera app of the iPhone 15 Pro makes it easy to follow the Rule of Thirds. A series of lines will appear on your screen when the grid is enabled in the camera settings, assisting you in aligning your subject and other items in accordance with the guideline. Whether you're photographing ordinary settings, landscapes, or portraits, this method may help your pictures have a feeling of balance and harmony.

How to Make the Grid Active:

1. Launch the iPhone's Settings app.

2. Hover your cursor over Camera.

3. When use the camera app, toggle on Grid to activate the overlay.

Violating the Third-Range Rule

Although the Rule of Thirds is a useful guideline, some of the most striking images are produced by purposefully defying it. After you know how to apply the rule, you may play around with it by putting objects close to the boundaries of the frame, centering your subject, or use symmetry to emphasize unusual viewpoints or generate tension.

Innovative Framing Strategies Going Beyond the Third-Party Rule

1. Patterns and Symmetry

In photography, symmetry creates harmony and order. You may symmetrically frame your subject by using architectural or natural characteristics, with the main point situated in the middle of the picture. This method works particularly well for photos of buildings, reflections, and landscapes.

2. Headlines

the primary topic of the photograph is guided toward it by leading lines. These lines might represent the horizon, highways, rivers, or even paths. The wide-angle lens of the iPhone 15 Pro is ideal for capturing strong leading lines that improve composition.

3. The Frame Inside the Frame

This method is framing your subject using man-made or natural elements, such as windows, entrances, or tree branches. It draws attention to the topic while giving the image depth and context.

4. The Negative Space

the open or vacant spaces around your topic are referred to as negative space. You may create breathing room in your images and make the topic stand out by using negative space. This method may produce feelings of serenity and simplicity, so highlighting the primary topic more effectively.

5. The Fibonacci Spiral Golden Ratio

A more sophisticated compositional method that has been utilized for ages by artists and builders is the Golden Ratio. While it adheres to a spiral pattern that naturally directs the viewer's attention toward the focal point, it is comparable to the Rule of Thirds. It's worthwhile to explore with the Golden Ratio since, according to some photographers, it produces a more harmonious composition than the Rule of Thirds.

6. Composition of Diagonals

Images gets dynamic character and a feeling of motion and energy when pieces are arranged diagonally. When attempting to evoke a feeling of movement or in action shots, diagonal compositions work very well.

7. Foreground and Depth of Field Elements incorporating foreground items into your images may enhance their depth and create a more immersive composition. You may produce amazing photos where the subject is well focused and the backdrop and foreground artfully fade out with the iPhone 15 Pro's sophisticated depth control.

8. Equilibrium and Asymmetry
it is not necessary for every photo to have perfect symmetry. When used well, asymmetry may provide a balanced but dynamic picture. This method usually entails putting the subject off-center and using contrasting colors, textures, or light and shadow to balance the remainder of the frame.

USING DEPTH AND PERSPECTIVE IN YOUR SHOTS

In photography, perspective and depth are essential components that may turn a boring picture into a composition that is interesting and dynamic. You may give your photographs additional levels of significance and visual appeal to make them more intriguing and appealing by comprehending and putting these concepts into practice.

1. Recognizing Depth

The appearance of three-dimensional space in an image is referred to as depth. Take into consideration the following methods to add depth:

• Background, Foreground, and Middle ground: In order to provide a feeling of spatial separation, include components in these three tiers. One way to create depth to your photo is to include an intriguing item in the front, a subject in the middleground, and a beautiful backdrop in the distance.

• Leading Lines: Make use of lines that entice the audience to focus on the situation. Roads, fences, and natural features like rivers and tree branches may all be examples of this. Leading lines highlight the scene's depth and aid in guiding the viewer through the picture.

• Overlap: Arrange items such that they partly block each other's vision. By establishing a spatial link between the parts, this approach helps to give the scene a more realistic, three-dimensional appearance.

2. Gaining Perspective Mastery

Perspective affects how items seem to relate to one another and may drastically change the way your shot is composed. Here's how to use perspective skillfully:

• Modifying Your Viewpoint: Try varying your perspectives and angles. While a high perspective might convey a feeling of remoteness or weakness, a low angle can make figures look bigger and more menacing.

• Disappearing Points: The intersection of parallel lines is a vanishing point. This method gives a strong feeling of depth and direction, which makes it very useful for taking pictures of buildings or highways and railroads.

• Wide-Angle Lens: When using a wide-angle lens, perspective may be emphasized, making things look bigger and further away from the camera appear smaller. This lens works well for taking pictures of large landscapes or interiors of buildings.

3. Making Use of Depth of Field Depth of Field (DoF) is the range of distance in a picture that seems to be reasonably crisp. You may improve your photographs' impression of depth by adjusting the depth of field:

• Shallow Depth of Field: To get a shallow DoF, use a wide aperture (f/2.8, for example). This method blurs the foreground and backdrop to provide depth while isolating your topic to make it stand out from the background.

• Deep Depth of Field: To get a deep DoF, when the background and foreground are both in focus, use a small aperture (f/11, for example). When taking landscape photos, this is perfect since you can catch every little detail in the picture.

4. Useful Advice for Incorporating Perspective and Depth

• Employ Foreground items: You may frame your subject and heighten the impression of depth by using foreground items such as flowers, pebbles, or textured surfaces.

• Play Around with Composition: Don't be scared to attempt unusual compositions and angles. Experimentation may often be the most effective method to find a persuasive viewpoint.

• Be Aware of Lighting: The way that depth and perspective are perceived may be influenced by lighting. Make the most of natural light and think about how highlights and shadows add dimension to your image.

HOW TO FIND THE BEST ANGLES FOR STUNNING PHOTOS

Selecting the ideal perspectives for striking photographs requires a combination of subject-specific knowledge, artistic vision, and technical proficiency. Here are some pointers to help you take impactful pictures:

1. Be Familiar with the Topic • Research the Topic: Recognize the special qualities and traits of your topic, whether it be an item, a person, or a landscape.

• Context Is Important: Think about how your topic is complemented or contrasted with its surroundings.

2. Try Out Various Angles of View

• Eye Level: Offering a natural perspective of the topic, this is the easiest angle to use and often the default selection.

• High Angle: Photographing a scene from above might provide the impression of dominance or provide a distinctive perspective.

• Low perspective: Using this perspective, your topic will seem more dramatic or forceful.

• Dutch Angle: Raising the camera's angle might evoke anxiety or tension.

3. Apply the Thirds Rule

• Grid Technique: Visualize two horizontal and two vertical lines dividing your picture into nine equal portions. For a composition that is balanced, arrange important pieces along these lines or at their intersections.

4. Experiment with shapes and lines

• Leading Lines: To direct the viewer's attention to the focal point or farther into the picture, use either natural or artificial lines.

• Geometric forms: Use forms to organize your composition and provide visual intrigue.

5. Think About Lighting

• Golden Hour: The gentle, warm light that appears in the early morning or late afternoon gives off a lovely glow.

• Backlighting: Dramatic silhouettes may be produced by positioning your subject in between the light source and the camera.

• Side lighting: Aids in drawing attention to features and textures.

6. Use Background and Foreground Elements

• Depth: A feeling of depth and context may be produced by including things in the front.

• backdrop: Make sure the backdrop draws attention to the topic rather than detracting from it.

7. Employ mirrors and reflections

• Water Surfaces: Puddles, lakes, and ponds may provide lovely symmetry and reflections.

• Mirrors: They may quadruple the visual attraction and provide a unique twist.

8. Play with Patterns and Symmetry

• Symmetry: Visually arresting and aesthetically beautiful compositions may be centered or balanced.

• Patterns: Adding recurring features or patterns to your images may give them rhythm and appeal.

9. Inspect or Observe

• Close-Up Shots: Get up close to your

subject to capture textures and details.

• Wide Shots: To provide context, show the topic in its entirety or take a picture of its surroundings.

10. Employ a stabilizer or tripod

• Stability: A tripod or stabilizer may assist reduce camera shaking for crisp and clear photos, particularly in low light or with extended exposures.

11. Review and Modify • Preview Your Shots: Examine your photos and, if necessary, change the viewpoint. A little adjustment may sometimes have a significant impact.

• Practice: To acquire an eye for what works best for diverse subjects and settings, experiment with varied perspectives on a regular basis.

CHAPTER 4

LIGHTING TECHNIQUES FOR IPHONE PHOTOGRAPHY

UNDERSTANDING NATURAL VS. ARTIFICIAL LIGHT

Light is a vital component that affects how we see and take pictures in both daily life and photography. Knowing the distinctions between artificial and natural light might help you make wiser choices in both situations. Natural light is defined as light that originates from the sun. Direct sunshine and diffused light that has been dispersed by fog, clouds, or other meteorological conditions are both included.

Features:

1. Color Temperature: Throughout the day, natural light changes. at golden hour, which occurs at dawn and sunset, it has a warmer

tone; at noon, it has a cooler tone. Natural light's color temperature is expressed in Kelvin (K), with midday light being between 5,000 and 6,500K and early morning and late afternoon light being between 2,000 and 3,000K.

2. Direction and Intensity: As the sun travels across the sky, natural light changes in both direction and intensity. Warm tones and extended shadows are produced by the softer, more angled light of the early and late afternoon. Shorter shadows and colder tones are produced by the harsher, more direct light of midday.

3. Quality: Direct or diffuse natural light is available. When sunlight is dispersed by clouds or other objects, it produces diffused light, which produces a softer, more uniform lighting. A clean, unhindered sun produces direct light, which produces striking contrasts and crisp shadows.

Uses:

• Photography: Take use of the warm, soft

light that the golden hour provides to accentuate colors and soften sharp shadows. Diffused light may provide a smooth, pleasing lighting for portraiture.

• Interior Design: Making the most of the natural light in a space may make it seem cozier and more open. Using light curtains or placing furniture close to windows might assist maximize natural light.

Definition of artificial light: Any light source produced by humans, including LEDs, lamps, and bulbs, is referred to as artificial light. It may be used in lieu of or in addition to natural light.

Features:

1. Color Temperature: The color temperature of artificial light sources varies and is often expressed in Kelvin (K). Warm light is produced by incandescent bulbs (2,700K), while cool white (4,000K) to daylight (6,500K) may be achieved with LED and fluorescent lights. A space's look and mood may be influenced by its color temperature.

2. Direction and Intensity: Compared to natural light, artificial light is more precisely controllable. Diffusers, reflectors, and dimmers may be used to control its direction and intensity. This adaptability enables personalized lighting configurations.

3. Quality: The kind of light source determines the artificial light's quality. Incandescent lights give off a softer, warmer glow, but LEDs and fluorescent lights may be harsh if they are not diffused appropriately. Natural light conditions may be replicated or simulated using high-quality artificial lighting.

Applications: • Photography: Adjust the exposure and atmosphere of a scene using artificial lighting. Whether you want to create dramatic contrasts or simulate natural light, studio lights, soft boxes, and reflectors may help you get the desired image.

• Interior Design: You may improve a space's beauty and usefulness using artificial lighting. An ambient, task, and accent lighting system may be made to be both well-balanced and adaptable by layering several lighting sources.

Blending Artificial and Natural Lighting

The finest outcomes are often obtained by blending artificial and natural light sources. For instance, continuous and adaptable lighting may be achieved by using natural light throughout the day and adding artificial lights for nighttime or low light situations. Combining the two light sources in your photographs may provide interesting effects and help you achieve a balanced lighting setup.

Knowing how artificial and natural light works may help you make wise choices in a variety of situations, from taking beautiful pictures to creating places that are both visually pleasant and useful.

HOW TO USE THE IPHONE'S NIGHT MODE FOR LOW-LIGHT PHOTOGRAPHY

The iPhone's Night Mode function is an effective tool for taking beautiful pictures in dim light. This technology, which was first included in the iPhone 11 and improved upon in later generations, senses when there is not enough light and turns on automatically to help you snap better, more detailed pictures at night or in low light. Here's a detailed tutorial on making efficient use of Night Mode:

1. Recognizing the Night Mode
Night Mode uses sophisticated computational photography algorithms to improve your images taken in low light. It creates a single, properly exposed picture by stitching together numerous frames that were shot over a few seconds. This enhances detail and clarity while lowering noise.

2. Activating the Night Mode
when the iPhone senses low light, it

immediately enters Night Mode. When Night Mode is enabled, a moon icon with a star symbol will appear in the upper left corner of the Camera app screen. In the event that the symbol is absent, the existing illumination circumstances do not need the use of Night Mode.

3. Modifying the Exposure Duration

You may manually change the exposure duration in Night Mode to fit your needs:

• Press the moon symbol: There will be a slider that lets you adjust how long the exposure is for. This slider allows you to change the exposure time; the iPhone will automatically recommend a duration depending on the available illumination.

• Lengthier exposures: To catch more light in gloomy environments, you may need to use a longer exposure period. If the subject or camera moves during the shot, be aware that motion blur may occur.

• Shorter exposures: To prevent excessive blur and preserve picture quality in somewhat dimmed settings, a shorter exposure could be enough.

4. Maintaining Your iPhone Stable

Motion blur may be avoided by keeping your iPhone as still as possible, as Night Mode entails longer exposure periods. Here are some pointers:

• Employ a tripod: This will steady your iPhone and enable longer exposure periods without any trembling.

• Lean on a firm surface: To lessen camera shaking in the absence of a tripod, consider leaning against a wall or resting your elbows on a sturdy surface.

• Set a timer: To prevent any movement when you push the shutter button, set a timer. This may guarantee a photo that is clearer.

5. Organizing Your Shot Even in low light photography, composition is crucial. Think about the following:

• Pay attention to intriguing details: Make sure your photo's primary subjects are positioned correctly within the frame.

• Look for anything distracting: Check for any reflections or strong lighting that might make your shot seem less good.

6. Editing and reviewing

following the capture of your Night Mode image: • examine the image: Verify the picture to make sure it lives up to your expectations. The picture produced by Night Mode need to be sharp and well-lit.

• Adjust as needed: Adjust the exposure, contrast, and sharpness using the Photos app or other third-party editing tools. The finished product may be made better by enhancing details or changing the brightness. These instructions will help you get the most out of your iPhone's Night Mode so you can take amazing pictures in low light. Try out various configurations and methods to see which suits your particular shooting situations the best.

CONTROLLING EXPOSURE AND USING HDR

Mastering exposure and using HDR (High Dynamic Range) are critical abilities for taking beautiful pictures. Both features handle distinct areas of light and detail in your images to help you obtain the greatest possible quality.

Handling Exposure Your photo's appearance depends on how exposed it is. For improved outcomes, you may manually adjust exposure on the iPhone 15 Pro. Here's how to do it:

First, launch the Camera app. To begin, open the iPhone 15 Pro's Camera app.

2. Tap to Focus: Tap the region of the image that you want to draw attention to. Based on that focus point, this step also establishes the first exposure level.

3. Modify Exposure: After you press to focus, the focus box will be accompanied by an image of the sun. This symbol may be moved up or down to change the exposure. The picture will become brighter when dragged

up, and darker when slid down.

4. Lock Exposure: Press and hold the focus point until "AE/AF Lock" appears at the top of the screen to lock the exposure settings so that they don't alter when you move your camera. This is especially helpful for maintaining constant exposure under fluctuating illumination circumstances.

By combining many images taken at various exposures, HDR (High Dynamic Range) allows you to capture more information in both the bright and dark regions of a picture. Here's how to make efficient use of HDR:

To activate HDR, launch the Camera app and press the HDR symbol, which resembles a circle with three lines. You have the option of selecting from "Auto," "On," or "Off." Set it to "Auto" so that your iPhone will determine when HDR is required for the best results.

2. Take the Picture: Take your picture normally after turning on HDR. The iPhone will automatically snap many pictures at various exposures and stitch them together

to create a single picture.

3. Examine HDR Photos: When you take a picture with HDR turned on, your iPhone stores the original version of the picture as well as the HDR version. To decide which one you like more, you may examine both in the Photos app.

4. Manual HDR: If you like the appearance of a regular shot or are taking a scene with little contrast, you may wish to manually disable HDR in certain circumstances.

When to Apply HDR

• High Contrast settings: When taking pictures of settings that have a lot of contrast between light and dark elements, such a landscape with a brilliant sky and a dark foreground, HDR is very helpful.

• Low Light Conditions: When there is a noticeable variation in the scene's light levels, HDR may also be useful in low light.

• Detailed Textures: HDR makes sure you don't miss any significant features in the highlights or shadows while capturing fine details and textures.

CHAPTER 5

ADVANCED PHOTOGRAPHY TECHNIQUES

MASTERING PRORAW: WHEN AND HOW TO USE IT

With the iPhone 12 Pro, Apple unveiled the ProRAW format, which is a potent tool for photographers looking to shoot photos with the most flexibility and information possible. ProRAW combines the advantages of a raw picture format with the computational improvements of Apple's image processing, in contrast to regular JPEG or HEIC formats. We'll explore when and how to utilize ProRAW to improve your photos in this article.

ProRAW: What is it?

ProRAW is a file format that combines Apple's sophisticated computational photography improvements with the raw picture data straight from your iPhone's camera sensor. This means you receive the advantages of Apple's HDR, noise reduction, and color accuracy coupled with the freedom of editing raw data.

When to Apply ProRAW
1. High-Detail Scenes: ProRAW works best in scenarios when capturing minute details is essential, such in photographs of complex textures or landscapes. More scene data is preserved by the format, enabling more thorough alterations.
2. Low-Light Conditions: ProRAW may assist you in recovering information that regular formats could lose in low-light situations. Better noise reduction and detail improvement during post-processing are made possible by the extra data.
3. Flexibility in Post-Processing: ProRAW provides more flexibility if you want to make extensive picture adjustments. Compared to processed formats, raw data makes exposure, white balance, and shadow

adjustments more straightforward and efficient.

4. Dynamic Range: ProRAW preserves details in both highlights and shadows when taking pictures of situations with a lot of contrast between bright and dark regions. This is very helpful for taking pictures of high contrast settings, such as sunsets and sunrises.

5. Professional Work: ProRAW offers the quality and versatility required for advanced picture editing, making it ideal for anybody using their iPhone for work-related or leisurely purposes.

How to Utilize ProRAW
1. Turning on ProRAW
o Launch the iPhone's Settings app.
o Go to Formats > Camera.
o Turn on the Apple ProRAW. You have the option to leave it on or to switch it on and off as required.
2. To take ProRAW images, use the Camera application.

o Press the ProRAW symbol, which resembles a "RAW" emblem, in the upper-right corner of the display. It will become yellow to show that ProRAW is active.

o Take your regular picture. The ProRAW format will be used to save the picture.

3. Editing ProRAW Pictures: o Launch the Photos application, then choose a ProRAW picture.

o To access the editing tools, tap Edit. Taking use of the expanded data in the ProRAW file, you may modify exposure, contrast, brightness, and more.

OYou might decide to utilize third-party programs like Adobe Light room or Capture One, which provide greater control over raw files, for more complex changes.

4. Managing ProRAW Files: Make sure you have enough storage space since ProRAW files are bigger than JPEGs or HEICs.

o To avoid storage problems, think about periodically unloading or backing up your ProRAW images.

Some Advice for Using ProRAW Well

• Recognize Your Storage Limits: ProRAW files may use a lot of space. Take note of the storage capacity of your device and arrange your data appropriately.

• Develop Your Patience: Raw editing takes patience and expertise. To get the most of ProRAW, use the tutorials and practice often.

• Combine with Other methods: To get the best results, use ProRAW in conjunction with other photographic settings and methods. ProRAW used with either the Night or Portrait modes, for example, may provide some quite striking effects.

CAPTURING MOTION: ACTION SHOTS AND BURST MODE

Capturing the spirit of motion in photographs of dynamic situations or persons moving quickly may be an exciting and difficult task. The iPhone 15 Pro's Burst Mode and other motion-capturing capabilities, in particular, provide you tremendous tools to help you capture amazing action images. A tutorial on maximizing these tools is provided here.

A Potent Tool for Action Shots Is Burst Mode Burst Mode is meant to assist you in capturing subjects that move quickly by allowing you to take a rapid sequence of pictures. This ability comes in very handy when photographing animals, sports, or any scenario where the motion is erratic.

1. Utilizing Burst Mode:

o Open the Camera App: Turn on your iPhone 15 Pro and open the Camera app.

o Toggle Burst Mode: Press and hold the shutter button to enter Burst Mode. Up until you release the button, your iPhone will keep taking pictures.

o Review Your Shots: The Photos app allows you to go over the photos you shot in a quick burst. Navigate to the burst photo collection and use the swipe function to choose your favorite picture.

2. Choosing the Best Shot: o press "Select...": In the Photos app, press "Select..." to see every picture that was taken after choosing the burst shot.

o Select Your Favorites: Scroll through the pictures and touch the ones you want to save. You may choose one or more images from the burst sequence.

o erase the Rest: To clear up storage space, touch "Done" after selecting the pictures you want to save. This will erase the other files.

Advice for Optimizing Action Shots
1. Attention and Exposure
o Adjust Focus by Hand: Prior to initiating the burst sequence, tap on the subject to

establish attention. This guarantees that the moving object maintains its sharpness.

o Modify Exposure: To change the exposure, swipe up or down on the screen. Having the right lighting is essential to getting crisp, precise action images.

2. Make Use of Optical Image Stabilization (OIS): The iPhone 15 Pro has sophisticated OIS, which lessens hand-motion blur. To get the most out of OIS, make sure you keep your iPhone steady when taking action images.

3. Experiment with Different camera Angles and viewpoints: To give your action photos more depth and variation, try experimenting with various camera angles and viewpoints. A topic might look more lively and forceful from low angles.

4. Capture Motion Blur for Artistic Effect: o you may purposefully employ motion blur to imply speed and action. Use a slower shutter speed and maintain motion for this effect. The sophisticated algorithms of the iPhone 15 Pro contribute to the production of visually

beautiful and fluid motion blur effects.

5. Edit Your Action Shots: o To get the ideal outcome, crop the photos, change the colors, and add details using the built-in editing tools in the Photos app or third-party applications.

Advanced Functionalities: ProRes and ProRAW

The iPhone 15 Pro has ProRAW and ProRes formats for individuals who wish to shoot action images at a higher quality. These formats enable more thorough post-processing and provide more editing freedom.

• ProRAW: This format gives you more flexibility over exposure, color correction, and sharpening in post-processing by capturing photos with better detail and dynamic range.

• ProRes: Mostly used for video, ProRes may also be useful for taking comprehensive, high-quality motion sequences that you can edit later for creative projects or frame-by-frame analysis.

MACRO PHOTOGRAPHY: CAPTURING INTRICATE DETAILS

The intriguing area of macro photography explores the smallest aspects of the environment we live in. Macro photography enables us to investigate textures, patterns, and features that are often hidden from view by taking pictures of things at very close ranges. This is a thorough guide to learning macro photography, with a focus on the iPhone 15 Pro.

Comprehending Macro Photography Photographing subjects at a 1:1 ratio or higher—that is, with the subject appearing on the camera sensor at its true size or larger—is known as macro photography. This method works well for getting very detailed images of little things like flowers, insects, or commonplace items.

How to Begin Taking Macro Photos
1. Make Use of the Proper Tools

The sophisticated camera features of the iPhone 15 Pro improve macro photography. The smartphone has excellent close-up capabilities because to its updated lenses, which include the new Ultra Wide lens. Make sure you know how to use the iPhone's macro mode, which turns on automatically as soon as you approach your subject.

2. Make Macro Mode Active

To fully use the macro features of the iPhone 15 Pro, do the following: • Launch the Camera app and choose the Ultra Wide lens.

• As you approach your subject, the camera will switch to macro mode automatically.

• Use third-party applications with macro photography tools, such as Halide or ProCamera, for manual control.

3. Level Up Your Shot

Precision is necessary for macro photography. A little motion might cause your photo to become blurry. To keep your iPhone steady, place it on a sturdy surface or use a tripod. To prevent camera wobble, think about using the timer feature or a remote shutter release.

4. Pay Close Attention

getting a clear focus is essential for macro photography. Although the iPhone 15 Pro has very sophisticated focus capabilities, you may need to manually touch on your subject to get exact focus. To improve your chances of obtaining the ideal focus, take many pictures.

5. Make Use of Good Lighting

A key factor in macro photography is lighting. Although natural light is usually the ideal choice, artificial lighting may also be used if needed. Steer clear of bright direct light since it might produce undesirable highlights and shadows. To soften shadows, utilize a reflector or diffused light sources instead.

6. Test Your Depth of Field

A extremely small depth of focus is common in macro photography, which may accentuate the dramatic appearance of your subject. Try varying the aperture to adjust the depth of field. You can mimic this look with the iPhone

15 Pro by utilizing portrait mode to produce a blurred backdrop that draws attention to your subject.

7. Consider the Composition

In macro photography like in other forms of photography, composition is crucial. To produce visually attractive photos, use composition, leading lines, and the rule of thirds. Observe carefully the surrounding area and anything that might divert attention from your primary topic.

Using Photoshop to Edit Your Macro Images

After taking your macro photos, utilize editing software to make them even better. Numerous options are available for modifying exposure, contrast, sharpness, and color balance in apps such as Adobe Light room, Snapseed, and Apple Photos. Additionally, cropping might assist in drawing attention to the most captivating areas of your picture.

CHAPTER 6

VIDEO MASTERY ON THE IPHONE 15 PRO

INTRODUCTION TO CINEMATIC MODE

With its many potent features, the iPhone 15 Pro will help you take your photography and filming to the next level. Among them, Cinematic Mode is particularly noteworthy as a ground-breaking instrument that allows amateur video to be seamlessly blended with professional-caliber cinematography. With the ease of your iPhone, you can now produce films with a depth of field that can compete with Hollywood productions thanks to this function.

With Cinematic Mode, you can concentrate on your subject and artistically blur the backdrop by automatically creating a narrow depth of field using powerful computational photography and machine learning. This gives your films a polished and captivating look by emulating the look of expensive cameras used in cinema.

However, Cinematic Mode offers more than just gorgeous graphics; it also adds subtle emphasis shifts. The iPhone 15 Pro may either automatically change focus when a subject approaches the frame or let you make manual focus adjustments after the shot is taken. You may narrate tales more skillfully with this dynamic focus control, directing the audience's attention exactly where you want it.

In addition to supporting 4K resolution and HDR recording, this mode guarantees that your films will be rich in color and depth in addition to being masterfully constructed. Cinematic Mode on the iPhone 15 Pro offers a flexible and powerful tool to realize your vision, whether you're capturing unique moments, making short films, or producing content for social media.

We will go over how to master Cinematic

Mode in the next chapters, covering everything from knowing its settings and capabilities to using advanced methods to produce results on par with professionals. By the time you finish reading this article, you'll know how to fully use Cinematic Mode to turn your iPhone 15 Pro into a powerful tool for artistic expression.

CREATING SMOOTH VIDEOS WITH STABILIZATION AND FOCUS CONTROL

The sophisticated stabilization and focus control on the iPhone 15 Pro are two exceptional capabilities that may greatly improve the quality of your video shot. These tools guarantee that your movies seem clean and professional, regardless of whether you're shooting fluid dramatic shots or quick-paced action scenarios.

1. Making Use of Video Stabilization

A more advanced optical image stabilization (OIS) mechanism in the iPhone 15 Pro helps to reduce the impacts of camera shake. This is very helpful when taking handheld photos or when a tripod is not available. Videos are smoother and more steady as a consequence of the stabilization function, which makes up for little movements. How to maximize it is as follows:

• Turn on Stabilization: The iPhone 15 Pro has built-in stabilization, but you may manually check and tweak it in the camera settings if required.

• Maintain a Steady Grip: Using both hands to hold your iPhone and keeping your elbows close to your torso will help minimize shaking even with stabilization.

• Use a Gimbal or Tripod: If you want even smoother photos, particularly while you're moving, think about using a tripod or gimbal. The steadiness of your video may be substantially improved using these techniques.

2. Gaining Control Over Focus

A key component of filmmaking is focus, and the iPhone 15 Pro's sophisticated focus management tools let you get the right amount of depth and clarity in your shots.

• Tap to concentrate: To concentrate on your topic, just tap the screen. Sharpness will be guaranteed where you need it thanks to the iPhone 15 Pro's camera locking onto that spot.

• Focus Lock: Make advantage of this

function when you want to keep your attention on a certain location or in circumstances where the subject may move. Once you've tapped to focus, hold down the screen button until the "AE/AF Lock" notice appears. By locking both focus and exposure, this avoids unintentional changes while recording.

• Tracking Focus: The iPhone 15 Pro has a better tracking focus function that enables the camera to automatically maintain focus on moving objects. This is especially helpful in situations with a lot of movement, since it may be difficult to keep manual focus.

3. Using Focus Control and Stabilization Together for Cinematic Shots

Achieving cinematic video quality requires careful focus management in addition to stabilization. Here are some pointers:

• Slow Motion and Focus: To guarantee that your subject stays crisp throughout the movie, utilize tap-to-focus or focus lock. utilize stabilization to make your slow-motion film fluid.

• Dynamic Shots: Enable tracking focus to maintain focus on your subject while stabilization eliminates any jolts or vibrations for more dynamic movements, such as panning or following a subject.

• Manual Control: You may manually change the focus of a photo to draw the viewer's attention away from one topic and toward another if you're going for a more styled appearance. This method, called "rack focus," gives your films a polished appearance.

4. Post-Production Advice

Even after filming, post-production tools for focus and stability might help you improve your videos:

• iMovie and Final Cut Pro: These editing software programs from Apple provide further stabilizing capabilities to help any last jerky film become smoother. They also provide you more creative control over how you show your scenes by letting you change the focal points after you've shot.

• Third-Party Apps: Apps like as LumaFusion provide sophisticated settings for sharpening focus and stabilizing video, allowing you more artistic control over your editing. You may create visually striking films with the professional quality associated with high-end productions by learning how to utilize the iPhone 15 Pro's stabilization and focus control features. These tools will make sure your films stand out, whether you're shooting on location or meticulously arranging a set.

4K, 8K, AND BEYOND: CHOOSING THE BEST RESOLUTION FOR YOUR NEEDS

In the quickly changing fields of photography and video, resolution is essential to the overall quality, clarity, and detail of your work. The business went from 1080p Full HD to 4K as technology developed, and now 8K is gaining popularity. But how can you choose the ideal resolution for your requirements when there are so many possibilities available? To aid with your decision-making, let's get into the specifics of 4K, 8K, and beyond.

Gratitude Result

Resolution is the quantity of pixels in an image or video; it is often expressed as a width by height measurement (e.g., 3840 x 2160 for 4K). An picture with more pixels will have a better resolution and be more detailed. Smoother movies and sharper visuals are produced by higher resolutions, particularly when seen on bigger displays.

4K Clarity: Four times the resolution of 1080p Full HD, Current Standard 4K, sometimes referred to as Ultra High Definition (UHD), boasts 3840 x 2160 pixels. For many TVs, monitors, and even smartphones like the iPhone 15 Pro, it has become the new norm. Why Opt for 4K?

• Clarity and Detail: 4K provides a great deal more detail than 1080p, which makes it perfect for big displays and improves the viewing experience.

• Widespread Support: Since 4K is supported by the majority of content producers, streaming services, and gadgets, it is a sensible option for both professionals and consumers.

• Editing freedom: 4K offers more post-production freedom to photographers and videographers, enabling them to cut and zoom without compromising quality.

For those seeking a medium ground between excellent definition and cross-platform interoperability, 4K is ideal. It works very well for professional applications when quality is crucial, content development, and home entertainment.

8K Resolution: The Clarity of the Future

With 7680 × 4320 pixels, 8K resolution provides four times the resolution of 4K. This is an incredible improvement in clarity, offering an almost realistic immersive experience.

Why Opt for 8K?

• Unrivaled Detail: With its unmatched degree of detail, 8K is perfect for intricate projects like digital painting, architecture, and visual effects on big displays.

• Future-Proofing: Purchasing 8K equipment today will guarantee that your material is still relevant years from now as 8K becomes more widely used.

• Creative Potential: Professional photographers and filmmakers may extract 4K photos from a single 8K video frame, giving them a great deal of editing versatility. However, there are several difficulties with

8K. Not all systems or devices can now handle it, and it needs greater processing power and storage. Professionals that want the greatest quality possible or hobbyists who want to remain on the cutting edge should use it.

After 8K: What Comes Next?

Even though 8K is now the highest resolution available to consumers, technology is always evolving. Researchers and developers are already pushing the envelope of what is feasible by investigating 12K and beyond. Virtual reality, augmented reality, and other immersive technologies—which need even higher resolutions to offer seamless experiences—will probably be the main drivers of these improvements.

Future Perspectives:

• Content Creation vs. Consumption: In the near run, content producers will gain more from higher resolutions than consumers. For present, 4K and 8K resolutions are more than enough if you're producing video for a large audience.

• Storage and Bandwidth: Larger storage capacities and quicker internet connections are needed to support higher resolutions. Before taking the plunge, be sure your infrastructure can handle these demands.

Selecting the Best Resolution for Your Needs

A few variables determine which resolution best suits your needs:

• Goal: Are you producing or consuming content? Higher resolutions provide additional flexibility and future-proofing for multimedia development. 4K is a wonderful standard for consumption, while 8K is an alternative for the best possible experience.

• Budget: Generally speaking, better resolutions entail more equipment and storage expenses. Think about how much money you have to spend and whether the additional pixels are worthwhile.

• Screen Size: On bigger displays, 8K's advantages become most apparent. 4K may be enough if you're dealing with smaller monitors.

Ultimately, knowing your demands and the capabilities of each resolution will help you make the right decision—whether you go with 4K, 8K, or opt to wait for the next big thing. The distinction between these resolutions will become more hazy as technology develops, providing additional chances to see and experience the world in breathtaking detail.

CHAPTER 7

EDITING PHOTOS LIKE A PRO

INTRODUCTION TO THE IPHONE'S BUILT-IN PHOTO EDITOR

The powerful camera technology and user-friendly interface of the iPhone have made it associated with high-quality photography. But what really makes it unique is the strong integrated picture editor that turns the phone into a full-featured mobile photo studio. With only a few touches, the iPhone's photo editor may enhance your photographs, regardless of your skill level: novice taking fast snaps or expert trying to adjust your shots.

The Development of iPhone Capture
Apple has consistently pushed the limits of mobile photography since the iPhone's launch. The camera's capabilities have

improved with every new version, making it easier for consumers to take beautiful pictures. But getting the ideal photograph isn't the only thing to do; editing is essential to honing and polishing your photos. Acknowledging this, Apple has been progressively enhancing the tools for modifying photos that are right inside the Photos app, enabling everyone to do complex picture editing.

A Smooth Integration

The iPhone's integrated picture editor's smooth interaction with the Photos app is one of its biggest benefits. You may begin editing as soon as you snap a picture; there's no need to export your photos to other programs. This integration guarantees a seamless and easy editing experience while also saving time. The editing process is made as efficient as feasible by the meticulous organization of each tool in the editor's simple interface.

Essential Features for Editing

The picture editor on the iPhone has a number of fundamental capabilities that may be used for both simple and complex editing. Among them are:

• Auto-Enhance: Immediately enhance your shot by adjusting exposure, contrast, and other factors with a single touch.

• Filters: You may instantly alter the tone and mood of your picture by using a range of filters.

• Adjustments: Use precise controls to adjust brightness, contrast, sharpness, and other features.

• Cropping and Straightening: This technique makes it simple to highlight the most significant portion of your shot and straighten it for precise alignment.

• Markups: For artistic or educational reasons, immediately add text, shapes, or drawings to your images.

Advanced Tools for Editing

The iPhone has sophisticated features that are comparable to many desktop editing programs for anyone who want to become more involved in picture editing. Among them are:

• Selective edits: Make fine edits to certain portions of your image, such as bringing out the details in a subject's face while maintaining the integrity of the backdrop.

• Noise Reduction: To make low-light photographs seem cleaner, reduce graininess.

• Vignette: To highlight the focal point of your image, apply a bright or dark gradient around the periphery.

• Depth Control: To have more control over background blur (bokeh), adjust the depth of field in portrait photographs.

Destructive-Free Editing

The non-destructive editing option of the iPhone picture editor is one of its best features. This implies that even after you save your revisions, you can always go back to the original picture and make any necessary tweaks or changes. You may play

around with various appearances and styles
thanks to this function without worrying
about losing your original photo.

BEST THIRD-PARTY EDITING APPS FOR IPHONE

The App Store has a plethora of third-party applications that may help you improve your picture and video editing skills on the iPhone. Some of the greatest third-party editing applications for iPhone that you should take into consideration are listed below, regardless of whether you're a professional photographer, a social media aficionado, or simply someone who enjoys capturing and enhancing memories:

Firstly, Adobe Lightroom
When it comes to iPhone picture editing, Adobe Light room is a formidable tool. With its expert-caliber tools, you can precisely adjust exposure, contrast, highlights, shadows, and more. It has unparalleled superior color grading and noise reduction capabilities. Because Light room allows for RAW processing, it's a must-have program for professional photographers. Its compatibility

with Adobe's Creative Cloud further enables smooth device synchronization, guaranteeing that your adjustments are always available.

2. VSCO

Influencers on Instagram and mobile photographers also love VSCO. It has a large selection of filters that may give your images a distinctive and polished appearance. Basic editing features like exposure, contrast, and saturation changes are also included in the program. The best things about VSCO are how easy it is to use and how well-made its presets are—you can adjust them to fit your style. Additionally, the app has an integrated community where you can exchange work and get inspiration from others.

3. The Snapseed

Google created Snapseed, a feature-rich and intuitive photo-editing application with a wide range of capabilities. Snapseed contains everything from simple brightness and contrast alterations to more sophisticated capabilities like perspective correction, selective editing, and healing. Its "Control Point" technique, which enables exact edits to certain sections of a shot, is one notable feature. Snapseed is an excellent option for photographers who want to adjust their images since it allows RAW editing.

4. The darkroom

with its intuitive UI, Darkroom is a powerful and stylish editing program that provides sophisticated capabilities. It offers functions that are often seen in desktop applications, such as gradient masks, curves, and selective color. Fast speed is another feature of Darkroom, especially when handling big files or RAW photos. Batch editing is supported by the program, which may save photographers a ton of time when editing many images at once. Its iCloud connectivity makes managing and accessing your picture collection across devices simple.

5. The Afterglow

After light is a feature-rich and user-friendly editing program that blends robust editing capabilities with a user-friendly interface. In addition to sophisticated features like gradient overlays, curves, and selective color, it provides an extensive selection of filters, textures, and frames. For users who seek creative control over their modifications without being burdened by feature-overkill, After light is ideal. Additionally, the program supports RAW editing, so you can work with high-quality photos.

6. Picture Pixelmator

With a host of potent editing options, Pixelmator Photo was created especially for smartphone photography. It has functions including support for RAW data, color tweaks, and repair tools. One of Pixelmator Photo's best features is its auto enhance function, which uses machine learning to automatically enhance your photographs with a single press. Additionally, you may experiment with various adjustments without worrying about losing your original picture thanks to the app's non-destructive editing feature.

7. Procreate Pocket This software is mostly renowned for sketching, but it also has a lot of picture editing features, which is great for those who want to add creative touches to their photos. It lets you paint over your photographs with a variety of brushes, layers, and blending settings. This program offers a degree of creative flexibility that is difficult to obtain in other applications, making it ideal for individuals wishing to combine photography with digital art.

8. Filmic Pro (for editing videos)
Filmic Pro is an excellent software that transforms your iPhone into a professional video camera for individuals who are interested in video editing. Advanced manual controls, such as those for focus, exposure, white balance, and frame rate, are available. Additionally, Log V2 recording is supported by the app for a wider dynamic range and more adaptable color grading. For filmmakers and videographers who want to record

excellent footage straight from their iPhones, Filmic Pro is the perfect solution.

9. LumaFusion Video Editing Software

A professional-level video editing app that competes with desktop programs is called LumaFusion. It provides key frame animation, multiple track editing, and an extensive selection of effects and transitions. The app's user-friendly design makes it suitable for both novices and experts, and it enables 4K video editing. For those who want to edit films while on the road without compromising on quality or control, LumaFusion is ideal.

10. Using Touch Retouch

The primary function of the specialized program Touch Retouch is to eliminate extraneous items from your images. Touch Retouch simplifies the process of enhancing your photographs by removing distracting elements such as power lines, signs, and people with a few simple clicks. If you edit images regularly, this software is a must-have because of its ease and efficacy.

With the skills and capabilities available in these third-party iPhone editing applications, you can elevate your photography and filmmaking to new levels. This collection includes programs that are easy to use and strong enough for professionals as well as simpler options for beginners.

HOW TO USE FILTERS, ADJUST COLORS, AND ENHANCE DETAILS

With the powerful toolkit that the iPhone 15 Pro provides for photographers, you can edit your photos right on the phone. Your images may go from decent to amazing if you know how to employ filters, change colors, and improve details. This is a detailed tutorial for learning how to use these features.

1. Employing Screens

A photo's tone or mood may be quickly and effectively changed with the use of filters. With only a few clicks, the iPhone 15 Pro's several built-in filters may be activated.

• Using Filters: Open the image in the Photos app that you want to change, then choose "Edit." Select the filter icon (three overlapping circles) from the bottom editing toolbar.

• Selecting a Screen: Go through the various filters and see how your picture is altered by each one. Options include vibrant color upgrades (Vivid, Dramatic) and traditional black and white (Mono, Silvertone).

• Modifying Filter Intensity: The slider located underneath the picture allows you to modify the filter's intensity once you've chosen it. This lets you adjust the impact to your desired level of subtlety or drama.

Since filters don't do any damage, you may easily go back to the original image if necessary.

2. Modifying Colors

If you want to improve or alter the color balance of your photos, color correction is essential. The iPhone 15 Pro comes with a number of features to assist you in adjusting colors.

• Getting to the Color Adjustments: Press and hold the dial-shaped adjustment icon to enter Edit mode. Exposure, brilliance, highlights, shadows, contrast, brightness, black point, saturation, vibrancy, warmth, and tint are among the settings you'll encounter.

• Vibrance and Saturation: Adjust the saturation of your image to change the hue of each color. Conversely, vibrancy modifies the strength of softer hues, which is advantageous for emphasizing details without overpowering already brilliant regions.

• Warmth and Tint: Warmth modifies the hue of your picture by imparting a blue (cool) or yellow (warm) cast. Green and magenta tones may be adjusted using tint, which is helpful for adjusting skin tones or removing color casts caused by lighting.

By making these changes, you may highlight the actual hues in your picture or establish a certain tone.

3. Improving Specifics

reducing noise, highlighting textures, and sharpening the picture are all part of enhancing details.

• Sharpness: To enhance the definition of the edges of your shot, use the Sharpen tool located in the Adjustments menu. This may enhance the visibility of little details, particularly in photographs of landscapes or buildings.

• Definition: By enhancing midtone contrast, the Definition tool highlights details and textures. This works especially well in close-up and portrait photography.

• Noise Reduction: Your picture may have some noise or grain if it was shot in dim lighting. To smooth out these flaws without losing too much information, use the Noise Reduction tool.

It's crucial to strike a balance between these alterations to preserve your image's natural appearance and highlight its most significant aspects.

Combining Methods to Get Professional Outcomes

Try combining these strategies for optimal results. To establish the general tone, use a light filter first, then adjust the colors to heighten the atmosphere. To finish, refine and highlight specifics to make your shot more vivid.

Recall that nuance is the secret to excellent picture editing. Over editing might produce photos that don't seem natural. Remain light-handed at all times, and make sure to tap the picture while in Edit mode to compare your changes to the original. This will guarantee that your edits add to the image instead of taking away from it.

CHAPTER 8

ADVANCED VIDEO EDITING ON THE IPHONE 15 PRO

USING IMOVIE AND OTHER VIDEO EDITING APPS

When used in conjunction with the appropriate applications, the iPhone 15 Pro can turn unpolished footage into polished films of high definition. With the aid of iMovie and other video editing tools, anybody who likes to capture moments or is an aspiring filmmaker can easily create beautiful films with the iPhone 15 Pro. iMovie: The Ideal Companion for Novices Apple's own video editing tool, iMovie, is a great place for anybody interested in using their iPhone 15 Pro for video editing. It's easy to use, with a number of features that even novices can utilize and enough capabilities to produce excellent films.

• Simple Interface: iMovie's interface is intended to be simple to use. With a few easy motions, you can rapidly import films from your Photos collection, organize clips, and cut video. With timeline-based editing, you can easily visualize and manage your project from beginning to end.

• Themes and Templates: iMovie has pre-made themes and trailers that give your films a polished appearance. These consist of titles, soundtracks, and transitions, which let you establish a unified style without having to start from scratch.

• Complex Editing Tools: Although iMovie is a user-friendly program for beginners, it also has sophisticated features like picture-in-picture, split-screen effects, and green screen capabilities. In addition, you have the ability to add sound effects, modify audio levels, and smoothly transition between segments.

• Support for 4K Video: The iPhone 15 Pro's 4K camera works in unison with iMovie's support for 4K video editing. This guarantees that your films maintain their best quality from the point of capture to the point of export. Additional Video Editing Apps to Consider

Even while iMovie is a great program, there are a number of alternative video editing programs available in the App Store that may help you create even better films. Here are several that are worth looking into:

1. LumaFusion o Professional-Grade Editing: For iOS video editors who take their work seriously, LumaFusion is often considered the best software. With its multi-track editing feature, you may combine titles, effects, audio, and video. With tools like audio mixing, color correction, and keyframing, this feature-rich program is perfect for those who want to work on more intricate projects.

· Support for External Drives: LumaFusion can handle editing straight from external drives thanks to the iPhone 15 Pro's improved hardware, which is a big benefit for handling large 4K video files without taking up space on your smartphone.

· Advanced Export choices: LumaFusion provides you with a plethora of export choices, such as aspect ratios, frame rates, and resolutions, enabling you to customize your video for a variety of sites, such as YouTube and Instagram.

2. Adobe Premiere Rush o Cross-Platform Editing: If you have to alternate between editing on a desktop computer, an iPad, or an iPhone, Adobe Premiere Rush is ideal for you. You may begin editing on your iPhone and finish on your Mac or PC since your projects are synchronized across devices.

o Creative Tools: Premiere Rush comes with pre-made motion graphic templates, editable title templates, and a music library. It is intended to be a simple and effective tool for making films suitable for social media sharing.

o Integration with Adobe Creative Cloud: Premiere Rush easily connects with Creative

Cloud if you already use Photoshop or After Effects, enabling more sophisticated adjustments and improvements.

3. KineMaster o Multi-Layer Editing: KineMaster has many capabilities, including voiceovers, chroma keying, blending modes, and several video layers. YouTubers and social media influencers that want a strong editing tool portable are especially fond of it.

o Real-Time Recording: You may include some spontaneity into your editing process by using the app to capture audio and video in real-time. Real-time previewing of your modifications is another feature that is essential for accurate alterations.

o Asset shop: KineMaster offers an asset shop where you may buy more typefaces, effects, and transitions to expand your creative possibilities.

InShot is a social media-focused platform that was created with content makers for social media platforms in mind. Videos may be easily cropped and resized to meet a variety of aspect ratios, including 16:9 for YouTube, 1:1 for Instagram, and 9:16 for TikTok.

o Easy Editing Tools: With its ability to split, merge, and trim clips, InShot is an excellent tool for rapid edits. It also makes it simple to add flare to your movies with a large selection of filters, effects, and music tracks.

o User-Friendly Interface: InShot has an easy-to-use interface, which makes it a great option for anyone who want to rapidly produce professional movies without delving too far into intricate editing methods.

Advice on Making the Most of Apps for Video Editing

1. Make a shot plan: Consider the tale you want to convey before you begin shooting. Organizing your photographs can help you save time while editing and guarantee that you get all the images you need.

2. Use Transitions Cautionary: Although they may give your films a polished look, using too many can make them seem crowded. Maintain a smooth and consistent movie by

using just a few essential transitions.

3. Optimize for Your Platform: Be mindful of the distribution channels for your video. The duration, file size, and dimensions of videos vary depending on the platform. You may export films in a variety of formats to fit your requirements using the majority of video editing tools.

4. Experiment with Effects: To improve your video, don't be scared to play around with filters, color correction, and other effects. Small changes might have a significant impact on the finished result.

5. Practice: Video editing requires practice just like any other ability. To become better at editing movies, take some time to go over each app's capabilities, watch tutorials, and try out some various kinds of editing.

You have everything you need to make visually striking and distinctive films, including the iPhone 15 Pro and the best video editing software. These resources will support your creative vision, whether you're working on a short film for social media or a longer, more involved effort.

CUTTING, TRIMMING, AND ADDING EFFECTS TO YOUR VIDEOS

The iPhone 15 Pro has an impressive set of features for video editing that make it simpler than ever to produce high-caliber film directly from your phone. Learning the fundamentals of cutting, trimming, and effect addition will greatly improve your narrative in films, regardless of experience level.

slicing and trimming Videos

Basic video editing methods like cutting and trimming let you polish your movie by eliminating extraneous scenes and emphasizing its strongest points.

Cutting: Cutting allows you to delete or reorder clips from your video by splitting it into distinct chunks. Using the Photos app that comes preinstalled on the iPhone 15 Pro or more sophisticated editing tools like Final Cut Pro or iMovie for iOS, this can be accomplished with ease. Just drag the timeline to the desired cutting point in the video, then choose "Split" or "Cut" from the menu. This will produce independent clips that you may remove, rearrange, or change at whim.

Trimming: Reducing the length of a video clip at the start or finish allows you to concentrate on the most significant parts. This is especially helpful for getting rid of any unnecessary or dead space at the beginning or finish of your video. With the iPhone 15 Pro, you can trim a video by opening the Photos app, choosing your movie, tapping "Edit," then dragging the handles on each side of the timeline to change the beginning and ending positions. To save your edits if you're happy with the trim, choose "Done".

Enhancing Your Videos Using Effects

Using effects in your films may significantly alter their tone and aesthetic, resulting in a finished work that is both distinctive and captivating. The iPhone 15 Pro comes with a number of effects that you may use straight in the Photos app or with more sophisticated programs like Adobe Premiere Rush or LumaFusion.

Filters: You may use filters to alter your video's overall color tone. Applying the various built-in filters on the iPhone 15 Pro just requires a few clicks. These filters may be used to add atmosphere, transforming your film into something sleek and futuristic or warm and nostalgic. Open the video in the Photos app, choose "Edit," and then "Filters" to add a filter. Before using any filter, you may check how it looks on your video by previewing it.

Transitions: Using transitions gives your films a polished appearance by seamlessly transitioning from one clip to the next. Transitions whether they be a simple slide, a crossfade, or a more intricate 3D effect, may assist keep your movie flowing smoothly and keep viewers interested. Many transition effects are available in apps like iMovie, and applying them between movies is a breeze. Time-lapse and slow motion video playback are also possible with the iPhone 15 Pro. If you want to demonstrate growth over time, time-lapse photography may speed up long film, while slow-motion effects can highlight certain events and add drama. These effects may be added after editing or applied straight while using the iPhone's camera to record.

Text and Titles: Adding text or titles to your movie may help set the atmosphere, highlight key parts, or provide context. You can add customizable text overlays with different fonts, colors, and animations to iMovie and other editing tools.

Sound Effects and Music: Adding music or sound effects to your videos is a breeze with the iPhone 15 Pro. Sound is an essential component of any video. You may add a voiceover from inside the editing software, import your own audio files, or choose from the built-in sound effects on the iPhone. Just make sure you own the rights to any music you use, or that it is royalty-free.

Some Advice on How to Edit Videos Effectively

1. Keep It Simple: Steer clear of overdoing the effects in your video, since this may detract from the main point. Apply effects carefully so as not to overpower the narrative.

2. Retain Consistency: To guarantee a unified appearance and feel, keep your style constant throughout the whole video. This entails applying consistent effects, transitions, and filters to each of your clips.

3. Check Your Edits: After making any changes, always check your video to make sure the effects improve rather than take away from the finished piece and the edits flow well.

4. Export in High Quality: Make sure to export your video in the best quality when you're happy with the modifications. With the iPhone 15 Pro's 4K video export capability, you can present your work in breathtaking clarity.

AUDIO CONTROL AND ADDING MUSIC TO YOUR FOOTAGE

Audio is essential for producing visually spectacular and emotionally stirring videos. Whether you're making a straightforward vlog or a cinematic masterpiece, knowing how to manipulate audio and blend music into your movie is crucial. You have access to a potent tool with the iPhone 15 Pro that lets you improve the whole watching experience by adjusting the audio in addition to shooting excellent videos.

Recognizing Audio Control

Controlling your video's audio includes adjusting the volume, clarity, and balance of the sounds. This procedure is made simple and effective by the following functionalities available on the iPhone 15 Pro:

1. Manual Audio Adjustment: You may directly change the volume of the sound on

your device by using the manual audio controls. This is very helpful when shooting in locations with different noise levels. To make sure that your audience can clearly hear the discussion, you may, for example, turn down the background noise while boosting the voices in a scene where there is dialogue.

2. Live Audio Monitoring: You can hear precisely what your microphone is recording in real-time with the iPhone 15 Pro when you use Air Pods or linked headphones for live audio monitoring. This tool allows you to make quick modifications to eliminate unwanted noise or distortion, which is very helpful while recording in unreliable situations.

3. Reducing Wind Noise: Wind noise may be a big problem while shooting outside. Built-in wind noise reduction technology in the iPhone 15 Pro automatically filters out these unpleasant noises, maintaining the quality and professionalism of your audio.

4. Spatial Audio: Supporting spatial audio, which produces an engrossing, three-dimensional soundscape, is one of the iPhone 15 Pro's unique features. This function gives your video audio the impression of originating from many directions, which gives it more depth and realism when paired with compatible Air Pods.

Including Music in Your Videos

When used in video production, music may establish the mood, amplify feelings, and direct the viewer's experience. Including music in your film using the iPhone 15 Pro is a simple process:

1. Choosing the Correct Path: Selecting the appropriate track is the first step in incorporating music into your video. Think on the tone and subject matter of your video. Is it a tense, contemplative moment or a fast-paced action sequence? The music ought to

accentuate the desired emotional effect and go well with the images.

2. Using Royalty-Free Music: Make sure you have the correct permissions to utilize the song while choosing music. With the iPhone 15 Pro, you may pick from a huge selection of genres and styles without worrying about copyright violations since it gives you access to many royalty-free audio libraries.

3. Editing and Syncing Music: After choosing your song, you must alter it so that it matches your video. You can loop, fade, and clip audio files using the built-in editing features of the iPhone 15 Pro, which include iMovie and Final Cut Pro for iOS. The overall impact of your film may be greatly increased by timing the music to major scenes, cuts, and action sequences.

4. Modifying Audio Levels: It's important to strike a balance between the music and the other audible components in your film, such

the speech and sound effects. You may individually control the music track's volume on the iPhone 15 Pro to make sure it doesn't overshadow other noises. Ducking is another tactic you may utilize. In ducking, the music automatically dims when there is conversation or other background noise.

5. Including Sound Effects: Sound effects, in addition to music, may give your film a further level of immersion. The iPhone 15 Pro makes it simple to add sound effects, ambient noises, or footsteps to your movie, giving the viewer a more dynamic and rich audio experience.

6. Exporting and Sharing: You can quickly export your movie in a number of different formats and sizes after you've finished editing the audio and adding your music. The high-quality export capabilities of the iPhone 15 Pro guarantees that your video's audio and visual components will remain intact when shared on other platforms.

CHAPTER 9

MASTERING PORTRAIT PHOTOGRAPHY

CAPTURING STUNNING PORTRAITS WITH THE IPHONE'S PORTRAIT MODE

The iPhone's Portrait Mode has completely changed mobile photography by making it simple for consumers to take gorgeous, high-quality pictures. Since its introduction on the iPhone 7 Plus, this function has developed, using cutting-edge technology to produce stunningly blurred backgrounds, or "bokeh," that accentuate the subject.

Recognizing Portrait Mode

To create its effects, Portrait Mode combines hardware and software. The dual-camera system in the iPhone, or the sophisticated single-camera system on some versions, measures the separation between the subject and the backdrop. Next, a depth-of-field effect is applied, which blurs the backdrop while maintaining crisp focus on the subject. The outcome is an arresting picture similar to what you would get with a DSLR camera with a fast lens, where the subject becomes the focus point.

Selecting the Appropriate Topic

The topic is what makes a portrait so amazing. Make sure everything, whether it's a human, an animal, or even an item, is well-lit and arranged to accentuate its best qualities. The ideal option is usually natural light since it gives a gentle, steady lighting that enhances the depth illusion. Make sure the subject of your picture has a well-lit face and bright eyes to enhance the quality of the shot.

Setting Up and Organizing

Take into account the shot's composition while utilizing Portrait Mode. A useful rule of thumb is to split your frame into nine equal portions using two horizontal and two vertical lines. This is known as the rule of thirds. To produce a composition that is both balanced and captivating, place the subject at one of the crossings. Try experimenting with other angles as well. A higher angle may provide a softer, more delicate image, while a little lower angle may make your subject seem stronger.

Changing the Depth Control

Depth Control is one of the most sophisticated functions seen in later iPhone models. This lets you change the amount of background blur before and after the picture is taken. You may regulate the amount of background that is in focus by altering the aperture, which is expressed in f-stops. A higher f-stop (such as f/16) will bring more of the background into focus, while a lower f-stop (such as f/1.4) will produce a more noticeable bokeh effect. This allows you to have artistic control over how your portrait turns out in the end.

By using Portrait Lighting, users may create effects that mimic various studio lighting settings using iPhones. Natural light, studio light, contour light, stage light, stage light mono, and high-key light mono are among the available options. From modest additions that simulate gentle sunshine to dramatic, high-contrast lighting that isolates the subject against a black or white backdrop, each option produces a different impact. Try out different configurations to see which works best for your topic and desired tone.

Improving Yourself Portraits Using Photo Editors

The editing features on the iPhone let you make extra adjustments to your portrait after it has been taken. Exposure, contrast, and color balance may all be changed to improve the overall appearance. You may further fine-tune your picture by using the Photos app to adjust the Depth Control and Portrait Lighting effects after the shot.

Third-party software like Adobe Lightroom or Snapseed provide more sophisticated editing features, such selective tweaks, healing brushes, and sophisticated color grading choices, for individuals who want to take their portrait photography to the next level.

Useful Advice for Great Portraits

• Keep the Lens Clean: Smudges on the lens may soften the picture and make your subject less sharp. To guarantee clarity, wipe the lens before taking a picture.

• Keep Your Hands Still: In low light, blur may be introduced by even the smallest movement of the camera. Think about using a tripod or turning on the picture stabilization tools built right into the iPhone.

• Pay Attention to the Eyes: The eyes are often the most prominent element in portrait photography. They usually grab the attention of the viewer, so tap the screen to make sure they are in crisp focus.

• Pay Attention to the backdrop: Even if the backdrop is blurred in Portrait Mode, you should still pay attention to what's behind your subject. When feasible, use simpler backdrops since busy or distracting components might take away from the overall impact.

EDITING AND ENHANCING PORTRAIT SHOTS

With the iPhone 15 Pro, you can fully realize the potential of your photographs by editing and improving portrait shots. This is a thorough instruction on optimizing your portrait photography with post-processing:
1. Make use of the Photos app
for perfecting your portrait photos, the iPhone 15 Pro's Photos app provides a wide range of editing options.
• Modify Exposure and Brightness: To make sure your portrait is well-lit, start by modifying the exposure and brightness. Adjust any overexposure or underexposure using the "Exposure" and "Brightness" sliders.
• Contrast and Definition: Draw attention to the topic by enhancing the contrast. To highlight the portrait's delicate details, boost the definition.
• Vibrancy and Saturation: Increase vibrancy to bring out the colors of the subject while

maintaining natural skin tones, or decrease brightness for richer colors.

• Sharpness: Adjust the sharpness to bring out the details, but take care not to sharpen too much as this might produce undesired noise.

2. Utilize filters

You may use filters to drastically alter the appearance and mood of your photo.

• Portrait Filters: There are filters in the Photos app made especially for taking portraits. These filters may change lighting effects, give a chic ambiance, or improve skin tones.

• Custom Filters: If you want greater flexibility, make your own filters or modify ones that already exist to fit your preferred style.

3. Retouching Equipment

Tools for retouching portraits are included in the editing suite of the iPhone 15 Pro.

• Skin Smoothing: To smooth out the texture of your skin while maintaining its natural features, use tools. Refrain from over smoothing, since this may give the subject an unnatural appearance.

• Blemish Removal: Use the retouch tool to eliminate flaws or blemishes. To keep things seeming natural, be subtle.

• Brightening of the Eyes and Teeth: To add vibrancy and interest to the picture, brighten the eyes and teeth.

4. Make Use of Outside Apps

If you want to modify more complexly, you may use third-party applications from the App Store.

• Adobe Light room: Provides sophisticated editing capabilities, such as professional retouching tools, intricate color grading, and selective tweaks.

• Face tune: This program specializes in improving portraits by enabling precise retouching, skin smoothing, and adjusting face features.

• Snapseed: Offers a selection of editing tools, such as filters and selective changes to improve portraiture.

5. Modifying Backgrounds

To maintain the attention on the issue, think about altering the backdrop if it is distracting.

• Blur the backdrop: To make the subject stand out more, use tools to subtly blur the backdrop.

• Replace or Enhance Backgrounds: Using some programs, you may add artistic or polished elements to your portrait photographs by replacing or enhancing the backdrop.

6. Last Words

• Crop and Straighten: If the alignment of your portrait is improper, crop it to make it seem better.

• Use Vignettes: By darkening the margins of the portrait, a vignette effect may draw attention to the person.

7. Store and Distribute

Save your finished portrait if you're happy with the adjustments. You can save adjustments on the iPhone 15 Pro without

erasing them, allowing you to always go back
to the original if necessary.

USING DEPTH CONTROL TO ADJUST BACKGROUND BLUR

One of the most notable aspects of the iPhone 15 Pro's camera system is Depth Control, which lets users adjust the blurring of the backdrop in their images. By providing exact control over the depth of focus, this tool improves portrait photography and makes your shots seem more polished. To efficiently control background blur, utilize Depth Control as follows:

Recognizing Depth Control

With Depth Control, you may mimic the appearance of a shallower depth of focus by using a bigger aperture. The backdrop is blurred by this technique, making the subject more visible. This effect, a smooth and customizable blur, is produced by the iPhone 15 Pro using its sophisticated computational photography algorithms in conjunction with its LiDAR scanner.

The Use of Depth Control

1. To capture a portrait photo, first open the Camera app and choose the Portrait setting. For optimal effects, make sure you're photographing in well-lit environments.

2. Take Your Picture: o Keep your subject at a fair distance from the backdrop. Depending on the settings and distance from the subject, the iPhone 15 Pro's camera will automatically apply a preset background blur.

3. Modify Background Blur: o After shooting the picture, open the file you want to work on in the Photos app.

o Press "Edit" in the upper-right corner.

o Choose the "Depth Control" slider, which is often situated underneath the picture and looks like an f-stop symbol.

o To modify the background blur, slide the control. The blur will be reduced by moving the slider to the left, sharpening the backdrop. A more noticeable bokeh effect may be achieved by sliding to the right, which will enhance the blur.

4. Preview and Save: o Real-time previews of

the changes are available when you modify the Depth Control. Press "Done" to save the edited picture if you're happy with the blur setting.

Some Advice for Efficient Utilization

• Examine the Subject: Increase the blur to highlight your subject, particularly in scenes with a lot going on.

• Play around with Depth Control: Varying the blur amount may significantly change the tone and focal point of your image, so don't be afraid to try different settings.

• Dimness and Length: Make sure you have enough lighting and keep your subject far away from the backdrop for the best effects. When there are noticeable differences between the topic and backdrop, the iPhone 15 Pro's algorithms function optimally.

Typical Uses

• Portraits: Give individual or group photos a more solitary, polished appearance to enhance them.

For close-up macro images when you want

the primary subject to stand out vividly against a blurry background, use Depth Control.

• Creating creative shots: Play around with various blur settings to highlight background forms and colors.

CHAPTER 10

PHOTOGRAPHY WITH ACCESSORIES

MUST-HAVE ACCESSORIES FOR IPHONE 15 PRO PHOTOGRAPHY

The correct accessories may make all the difference when it comes to enhancing the photographic capabilities of your iPhone 15 Pro. The following is a list of essential accessories to improve your photographic experience:

1. Superior Lens Adhesives

Wide-Angle Lens: This lens widens your field of vision so you can photograph more of the scene in one go. Perfect for group shots and landscapes.

Macro Lens: Ideal for up-close shots, this lens lets you get the fine details of tiny things, including insects or flowers.

With the help of a telephoto lens, you may

have a closer look at far-off objects without compromising the quality of your images.

2. Tripod Compact Tripod: For steady images, particularly in dim lighting or extended exposures. A small, lightweight tripod is ideal for daily usage and travel.

Flexible Tripod: An adaptable choice with legs that can be adjusted to wrap around objects or be positioned in unusual ways, this tripod is perfect for vlogging and artistic pictures.

3. Camera Grip: This photography grip improves comfort and control while shooting, particularly on long exposures. Certain grips have extra features or shutter buttons integrated into them.

Gimbal Stabilizer: By stabilizing your iPhone 15 Pro and minimizing camera wobble, this device aids in the recording of fluid, cinematic video.

4. Lightweight Portable Lighting

LED Light Panel: Ideal for portraiture or low light situations, this lighting source offers uniformity and adjustability to enhance your images.

Clip-On Light: Small and simple to use, this add-on may improve illumination for up-close photos or selfies.

5. An external microphone

Lavalier Microphone: Perfect for capturing crisp audio during video interviews or shootings.

Shotgun Microphone: Ideal for reducing background noise in your recordings and obtaining crisp, focused audio from a distance.

6. Lens Cleaning Kit Microfiber Cloth: This is a necessary item to maintain your lens clear of fingerprints, smudges, and dust that might degrade the clarity of your images.

Lens Cleaning Solution: Keeps your lens in optimal condition and helps remove more difficult smudges.

7. Transportable Battery Pack

A high-capacity power bank guarantees that you won't run out of juice while shooting, enabling you to continue taking pictures and movies all day long.

8. Safeguard Case

Rugged Case: Provides defense against knocks, drops, and other physical harm while preserving convenient access to the camera on your iPhone 15 Pro.

Lens Protection Filter: Prevents dust and scratches on your camera lens without sacrificing picture quality.

9. Photography applications Pro Camera Apps: With applications that include creative effects, sophisticated editing options, and manual settings, you may improve your photography skills.

Editing Apps: With capabilities that match those of a professional editing program, programs like Adobe Light room, Snapseed, or VSCO may help you refine your photos.

USING TRIPODS, GIMBALS, AND LENSES TO ENHANCE YOUR SHOTS

Using Lenses, Tripods, and Gimbals to improve iPhone Photography

1. Support poles

A tripod is an essential equipment for taking steady, accurate pictures. It reduces camera shaking and blur, which is particularly helpful in low light situations when longer exposure times are required. Here's how to use a tripod to its fullest:

• Stability: To guarantee that your iPhone stays completely motionless, use a tripod. This is essential for getting crisp photos, particularly when utilizing short shutter speeds or in low light.

• Composition: Careful framing and composition are made possible with a tripod. To get the precise photo you want, you may carefully change the height and angle.

• Long Exposure: A tripod is necessary to take long-exposure photos, such as those of star trails or running water. It stabilizes your iPhone for the duration of the prolonged exposure.

• Remote Shutter Release: You may operate your camera remotely by pairing a tripod with an app, or many tripods come with a remote shutter release. By doing this, any vibrations brought on by physically pushing the shutter button are reduced.

2. Gimbals

Gimbals are essential for filming because they act as stabilizers, reducing shake in the shot. They work especially well in dynamic scenarios or pictures that move. Gimbals may improve your iPhone filming in the following ways:

• Smooth Video: Gimbals provide smooth, polished-looking video by using motorized stabilization to offset hand motions.

• Creative Angles: You may experiment with different pans and tilts and other filming angles and motions with a gimbal without sacrificing stability.

• Versatility: Feature-rich modern gimbals often include object tracking, which maintains focus on your subject while you move the camera. For interviews or action shots, this works well.

• Ease of operate: A lot of gimbals are designed to be simple to operate and quickly converted to various shooting modes, enabling a variety of artistic effects and fluid shot transitions.

3. Eyeglasses

Because external lenses provide a variety of focus lengths and effects, they may significantly increase the creative potential of your iPhone photos. Here are some examples of how using various lenses may improve your photos:

• Wide-Angle Lenses: Designed to fit more into the frame or for taking landscape photos, these lenses capture a wider perspective. Large group and architectural photography may also benefit greatly from them.

• Macro Lenses: These lenses enable very close-up shots, highlighting minute features of tiny objects like insects or flowers. They are ideal for catching small details and textures that are often lost on ordinary lenses.

• Telephoto Lenses: These lenses include a zoom feature that lets you take closer, more detailed pictures of far-off scenes. They are very handy for taking pictures of animals or people when you want to keep a safe distance.

• Fisheye Lenses: These lenses provide a distinctive, rounded look and a broad, distorted picture. They work very well for taking imaginative, dramatic pictures from an inflated point of view.

Putting Together Tools

When you skillfully mix these instruments, the magic really begins. For example, a gimbal combined with a wide-angle lens may provide fluid, lifelike video footage of active situations, while a tripod and telephoto lens offer steadiness while zooming in on far-off objects. By enhancing one another, these tools let you take your iPhone photography and filming to new heights.

THE IMPORTANCE OF LIGHTING GEAR FOR BETTER PHOTOS

One of the most important aspects of photography is lighting, which has a significant impact on an image's mood, texture, and overall quality. Even the most well-composed photograph might seem uninteresting in bad lighting, yet a poorly lit image can be made to look compelling. Here's why purchasing high-quality lighting equipment is crucial to taking excellent pictures:

1. Command of the surroundings

Natural light often conflicts with your eyesight or schedule and might be unexpected. With lighting equipment, you may precisely regulate the light source to provide the mood and effect you choose. Controlling lighting guarantees consistency and dependability in your work whether you're filming outside or inside.

2. Better Quality Images

By lowering harsh shadows and regulating brightness levels, lighting equipment contributes to the improvement of picture quality. Soft boxes, diffusers, and reflectors are useful tools for softening harsh shadows and producing a more attractive appearance. This is especially crucial for portrait photography, since gentle, equal lighting may draw attention to the subject's best features and minimize distracting shadows.

3. Inventive Adaptability

Artificial lighting cannot provide the same creative possibilities as lighting equipment. You may play around with different effects, such dramatic highlights, gloomy shadows, or even colored lighting, by experimenting with different kinds of lights, including flash, strobes, or LED panels. Photographers are better able to convey their own vision and style because to this freedom.

4. Reliable Outcomes

In work environments, uniformity is essential. For tasks that call for a certain appearance or feel, lighting equipment guarantees that you get the same results every time. In situations when uniformity among photos is required, such as studio photography or product shots, this consistency is particularly crucial.

5. Improved Efficiency in Low Light

Cameras often struggle to produce crisp, well-exposed pictures in low light. Lighting equipment may help with this issue by adding more light. In difficult lighting conditions, using external lights may help you get crisper, more detailed photos while eliminating noise and the need for high ISO settings.

6. Enhanced Post-Processing Productivity

The quantity of post-processing adjustment required is decreased with good illumination. Less editing is needed to alter exposure, contrast, and color balance in well-lit images. This saves time and preserves the integrity of the picture, since over editing may sometimes cause the quality of the image to deteriorate.

7. Dependability and Professionalism

Professional lighting equipment is a sign of dependability and knowledge for photographers who deal with customers. It proves that you are capable of handling a variety of shooting situations and are ready to provide excellent outcomes. Purchasing high-quality lighting equipment may improve your reputation in the business and shows how dedicated you are to your work.

CHAPTER 11

ICLOUD AND PHOTO MANAGEMENT

ORGANIZING YOUR PHOTO LIBRARY

Cleaning and organizing your picture collection is essential to having a productive and orderly digital workspace. Here's a thorough how-to on efficiently managing and arranging your picture collection:

1. Establish a Structured Folder System

• primary Folders: To begin, create primary folders labeled "Events," "Travel," "Family," "Work," etc. for general categories.

• Subfolders: Make subfolders for certain occasions or themes under each main folder, such "2024 - New York Trip" or "Summer Vacation."

2. Give Your Files Detailed Names

• Time and Place: Put the date and a short description in the file name, for example, "2024-09-08_Mountains_Sunrise.jpg."

Steer clear of generic names: Avoid using general names, such as "IMG_1234", since they might make it more difficult to find individual images later.

3. Put in Place a Tagging System • Keywords: Tag images with pertinent phrases like "sunset," "beach," or "birthday."

• People and Places: Tag individuals and places to facilitate finding, particularly in large picture collections.

4. Utilize information • Edit Metadata: Verify the accuracy of your photographs' information (also known as EXIF data). This contains the location, date, and time.

• Make Use of Software: To organize and classify your photographs, use photo management software that can read and use metadata.

5. Consistently Evaluate and Trash

• Eliminate Duplicates: Continually search for and eliminate duplicate images.

• Eliminate Undesired Images: To maintain your library clutter-free, get rid of any photographs that are hazy, unnecessary, or repetitive.

6. Backup Your Pictures • Cloud Storage: Set up automatic backups using cloud services like Dropbox, Google Photos, or iCloud.

• External Drives: To avoid data loss, periodically backup your picture collection to an external hard disk.

7. Make use of picture organizing software

• Apple Photos: Offering organizing features like folders, smart albums, and albums, Apple Photos is available for Mac and iOS users.

• Adobe Lightroom: Lightroom has sophisticated organizing tools including star ratings, groupings, and keywords.

8. Make collections and albums

• Curated Albums: Produce albums for collections with certain themes, such as "Family Portraits" or "Vacation 2024."

• Smart Albums: Utilize smart albums to automatically organize images according to keywords, location, or dates.

9. Uniform Naming Guidelines

• Standardize: To guarantee consistency and accessibility, name folders and files according to a consistent standard.

• Steer clear of special characters: To prevent problems with various operating systems, stick to letters, numbers, and underscores.

10. Make use of filters and search

• Search Functionality: To find certain photographs fast, utilize the search functions in photo management software.

• Filters: Use filters to arrange images according to categories, location, or date.

SYNCING AND BACKING UP YOUR PHOTOS AND VIDEOS

In the era of digital photography, it is essential to make sure that your images and movies are correctly synchronized and backed up. This is a thorough guide on organizing and protecting your priceless media:

1. Utilizing iCloud Images

Across all of your Apple devices, iCloud photographs is an Apple service that maintains your photographs and videos current. Here's how to make good use of it:

• Toggle on iCloud Photos on your iPhone 15 Pro by going to Settings > [Your Name] > iCloud > Photos. Your media will sync and upload to iCloud automatically as a result.

• Manage Storage: 5GB of free storage is available via iCloud. You may increase your storage plan via Settings > [Your Name] > iCloud > Manage Storage if you need extra space.

• Optimize Storage: Turn on Optimize iPhone Storage to save up space on your device. With this option, you may save the full-resolution copies of your images in iCloud and retain the smaller, optimized ones on your device.

2. Making Use of Google Photos

An adaptable substitute for backing up and synchronizing your images and movies is Google Photos:

• Set up the App: Open the App Store and download Google Photos. Launch the application and use your Google account to log in.

• Backup & Sync: Turn it on by going to Photos Settings > Backup & Sync. You have two options for upload quality: Original Quality, which has a greater resolution but is restricted by your Google Drive capacity, or High Quality, which offers free, unlimited storage (compressed).

• Organize and Search: Google Photos has robust search and organizing tools. You may utilize AI tools to improve and arrange your material, as well as make albums and do targeted picture searches.

3. Making Use of External Storage

For individuals who want more space or who would rather have actual backups:

• Outside Drives: To back up your images and movies, connect an external hard drive or SSD to your computer or Mac and use programs like File History (Windows) or Time Machine (Mac).

• Manual Transfers: Using File Explorer on a PC or the Photos app on a Mac, you may manually move images and movies from your iPhone 15 Pro to an external disk.

4. Making Use of Outside Backup Providers

Numerous outside providers provide reliable backup options:

• Dropbox: To automatically back up your images and videos, install the Dropbox app and turn on Camera Uploads.

• OneDrive: Using its mobile app, Microsoft's OneDrive also facilitates picture and video backups. In the app's settings, turn on Camera Upload.

• Amazon Photos: You can use Amazon Photos to save an unlimited amount of photos and up to 5GB of films if you're an Amazon Prime member.

5. Consistent Backup Procedures

• Arrange Backups: Plan backups on a regular basis to prevent losing recent material. While backups for iCloud happen automatically, you should schedule reminders for other services to make sure your backups are current.

• Verify Backup Status: Regularly monitor your backup configurations and storage utilization to ensure that your media is being appropriately backed up.

• Secure Your Accounts: To prevent unwanted access to your material, use strong, one-of-a-kind passwords and activate two-factor authentication for your backup services.

SHARING PHOTOS AND VIDEOS SEAMLESSLY ACROSS DEVICES

The foundation of digital convenience in today's connected society is the seamless sharing of images and movies across devices. The media transfer procedure between your iPhone 15 Pro and other devices is quick and easy, regardless of whether you're a professional photographer or simply trying to capture special moments. This is a thorough look at how to use this feature to its fullest: **1. iCloud Photos: iCloud Photos revolutionizes the way you can share and view your media on all of your Apple devices. Your images and videos are automatically synced across your iPhone, iPad, Mac, and even iCloud.com when you enable iCloud Photos. This makes it simple to view and share your files from anywhere by guaranteeing that any changes or new additions are quickly updated across all devices.

How to Turn on iCloud Pictures:

1. Open the iPhone 15 Pro's Settings.

2. To access your Apple ID settings, tap on your name at the top.

3. Choose Pictures from iCloud.

4. Turn on and off iCloud Photos.

**2. AirDrop: Airdrop is a great tool for exchanging images and movies across Apple devices quickly and easily. With just a few clicks, you can transmit media straight from your iPhone 15 Pro to another iPhone, iPad, or Mac.

Using AirDrop Instructions:

1. Launch the Photos application and choose the files you want to share.

2. Press the Share icon, which is an upward-pointing square.

3. From the list of nearby devices, choose AirDrop and select the recipient's device.

4. A message inviting the recipient to accept or reject the transfer will be sent.

**3. Shared Albums: Working on projects together or sharing with a group is made easier with iCloud's Shared Albums function. You have the ability to create shared albums that allow other people to see, like, and add their own images and videos.

How to Make an Album That's Shared:

1. Select the Albums tab after opening the Photos app.

2. Press the plus sign ( ) and choose "New Shared Album."

3. Give your album a name and provide the phone number or email addresses of anyone you would want to invite.

4. You may include images and videos in the album, which will be accessible to all members of the shared group.

**4. Messages and Mail: You may also immediately share media using Mail or iMessage. For rapid sharing with individuals or small groups, this is helpful.

How to Message and Share:

1. Launch the Photos application and choose the files you want to share.

2. Click the Share button, then choose

Messages.

3. Enter a phone number or choose the recipient from your contacts.

4. Send and, if wanted, add a message.

How to Distribute via Mail:

1. Launch the Photos application and choose the files you want to share.

2. Press the Share button, then choose Mail.

3. Before sending, enter the email address of the intended recipient and any other relevant information.

**5. Third-Party applications: Third-party applications with cross-platform sharing features, such as Google Photos, Dropbox, and OneDrive, are useful for users who switch between different devices and platforms. Using these applications, you may share or view your material from almost any internet-connected device by uploading it to a cloud server.

Using Google Photos: A Guide

1. Open the App Store, download, and install the Google Photos app.

2. Launch the app and log in using your Google credentials.
3. Store your movies and images on the cloud.
4. Use the Google Photos app to share content or view your media from any device.

CHAPTER 12

TAKING YOUR PHOTOGRAPHY TO THE NEXT LEVEL

CREATIVE PHOTOGRAPHY CHALLENGES TO SHARPEN YOUR SKILLS

Creative photo challenges are a great opportunity to hone your abilities and explore new creative avenues. The following interesting tasks can help you develop as a photographer:

1. Photo Challenge with a theme

Select an overarching subject, such "Reflections," "Minimalism," or "Urban Landscapes," then capture images that are consistent with this concept. This assignment pushes you to consider how best to capture the core of the topic while assisting you in concentrating on certain areas of photography.

2. One Week, One Lens

Use one lens—a wide-angle, macro, or telephoto lens—only once a week for a week. This constraint makes you use that lens to the fullest extent possible and modify your shooting approach to take advantage of its advantages and disadvantages.

3. Photographic Diary Every Day

Make a commitment to capture something interesting with your camera each day for a month. In addition to enhancing your technical proficiency, this regular practice helps you develop an acute sense of interest in themes and compositions.

4. The Challenge of Color Palettes

Select a color scheme and take pictures that mostly use that color scheme. You are urged to consider color harmony and the relationships between various hues in your compositions by this challenge.

5. Photographing Silhouettes

Take powerful pictures with only silhouettes

by placing your subjects in front of bright windows or sunsets, for example. This assignment highlights how crucial form and shape are to your compositions.

6. Taking Pictures in Low Light

Investigate the field of night or low light photography. Try varying ISO settings, long exposures, and lighting strategies to bring out the most in your subject's low light photography.

7. Take a Selfie

Make a bunch of self-portraits using various settings, lighting, and style options. In addition to being a fun opportunity to play around with your own picture, this challenge teaches you about lighting, composition, and emotion.

8. Photographing in Black and White

During a designated time, take black and white photos with an emphasis on forms, textures, and contrasts. This exercise focuses on the components that make powerful monochromatic visuals and helps you look beyond colors.

9. Using Photographs to Tell Stories

Make a sequence of images that narrates a story or conveys a message. This may be someone's day in their life, a trip, or an occasion. You can better consider visual sequencing and emotional effect by taking on this task.

10. Close-up Images

Use macro photography to explore the minuscule aspects of your surroundings. Take close-up pictures of commonplace items or natural features to examine often-overlooked textures, patterns, and little details.

Each of these tasks may push you to try out novel angles and ways while also helping you hone a variety of photographic talents.

EXPLORING MOBILE PHOTOGRAPHY COMMUNITIES AND CONTESTS

Communities and competitions are essential in the dynamic world of mobile photography for encouraging innovation, disseminating information, and winning recognition. These sites are a priceless resource for iPhone photographers looking to further their craft, show off their work, and pick up new techniques.

Communities for Mobile Photography

1. Social media groups and online forums:

o Instagram: A photographer's paradise, Instagram's expansive network lets you interact with a worldwide audience, follow hashtags pertaining to mobile photography, and network with other aficionados.

o Reddit: You may find forums, discussion threads, and places to exchange advice and techniques on subreddits like r/iphonephotography and r/mobilephotography.

o Facebook Groups: iPhone photography-focused groups provide a helpful setting for exchanging work, posing queries, and taking part in competitions.

2. Specific Mobile Photography Platforms: o EyeEm: This platform lets users share their photos, interact with other photographers, and take part in well planned photo missions. o 500px: This site offers a vibrant community for mobile photographers to share and get exposure for their photos, albeit it's not only for that purpose.

3. Local groups and Workshops: o Meetup.com: Use this platform to find local photography groups and make connections with people nearby. These events often include cooperative photo sessions and interactive workshops.

o Photography Clubs: A lot of places have clubs for photographers that accept traveling photographers and provide networking opportunities, seminars, and critiques.

Contests for Mobile Photography

1. Platform-Distinct Competitions:
o Instagram Contests: Influencers and brands often hold picture competitions on Instagram, usually with a focus on certain challenges or themes.
o EyeEm competitions: EyeEm often hosts competitions with a variety of topics, giving participants the opportunity to win rewards and increase their profile.
2. Photography Magazines and Websites: o The annual Mobile Photography Awards honor the top mobile photographers in a number of categories.
o National Geographic Your Shot: This competition welcomes all forms of photography, although it often has sections honoring mobile shooters.
3. App-Based Competitions: o Prisma: renowned for its creative filters, Prisma sometimes arranges competitions that include original edits created with their app.
o VSCO: On occasion, VSCO hosts competitions showcasing inventive use of

their editing software.

Success Advice

1. Take an Active Part: Take part in conversations, provide helpful criticism, and interact with the community. Developing connections may result in beneficial alliances and teamwork.

2. Stay Current: Keep abreast of developments and trends in the field of mobile photography. Staying up to date and creative may be achieved by being informed of current trends and methods.

3. Display Your Best Work: When entering competitions, make sure your best photographs fit the topic or criteria of the event.

4. Take Note of Feedback: Growth-oriented feedback is an effective instrument. Refine your talents with feedback from community interactions as well as competitions.

You may improve your abilities, get recognition, and make connections with like-minded people by becoming involved in mobile photography groups and competitions.

FINAL TIPS FOR MASTERING IPHONE PHOTOGRAPHY

1. Recognize Lighting: Proper lighting is essential for taking pictures. Aim to take pictures during the golden hours, which are just after dawn and just before sunset, since natural light is often the greatest. Place your subject close to windows if you're shooting inside for soft, diffused light. Steer clear of the intense noon light, which may produce awkward shadows.

2. Make Use of the Grid: To assist you in adhering to the rule of thirds, activate the grid in the camera settings on your iPhone. With the aid of this grid, which splits the frame into nine equal sections, you may better compose your shots and increase their visual interest.

3. Experiment with Angles: Take shots at angles other than eye level. To discover the most fascinating photo, experiment with various views and angles. To add variation to

your shots, go down to the ground, take pictures from above, or locate unusual vantage points.

4. Make use of the focus and exposure controls. To alter exposure, swipe up or down after tapping on your subject. This guarantees that your subject is crisp and well-lit, particularly in challenging lighting circumstances.

5. Make utilize of the Portrait Mode: To get amazing portraits, utilize the Portrait mode to blur the backdrop and highlight your subject by using a narrow depth of focus. Try out the various lighting effects in Portrait mode to get a range of outcomes.

6. Investigate the Editing features: Utilize the Photos app's editing features after taking your pictures. To improve your photos without going overboard, play about with the brightness, contrast, and color saturation settings.

7. Use Burst Mode for Action Shots: Burst mode allows you to quickly take many frames

in succession when taking pictures of moving objects. This improves your chances of capturing the ideal moment with the least amount of motion blur.

8. Maintain a Clean Lens: Sharp, clear photos are guaranteed with a clean lens. Using a microfiber cloth, clean the lens often to get rid of any fingerprints, dust, or smudges that can degrade the clarity of the picture.

9. Use a Tripod for Stability: Using a tripod may assist assure clear photographs and minimize camera shaking during long exposures or low light photography. Tripods that are small and reasonably priced are readily available and ideal for taking photos on the go.

10. Practice Often: Consistent practice is the greatest approach to enhance your photographic abilities. Try out various methods, go over your shots, and take away lessons from each encounter to keep improving.

CHAPTER 13

CONCLUSION

REFLECTING ON YOUR IPHONE PHOTOGRAPHY JOURNEY

Taking up iPhone photography is a journey that involves more than simply learning how to take amazing photos; it's also about expressing your creativity, capturing special moments, and becoming proficient with a device that fits neatly in your pocket. When you look back on your experience with iPhone photography, keep the following in mind:

1. Initial Curiosity and Exploration: You probably started on your trip out of curiosity. Perhaps you intended to take a picture of a stunning sunset, an intimate moment, or an artistic composition. Your development began with early exploration with the

photography functions of your iPhone. Think back to your early exploratory days. What motivated you? How did your comprehension of the iPhone's features change over time?

2. Learning and Development: As you became more proficient at iPhone photography, you started to understand the subtleties of editing, lighting, and composition. Recall the tools you used, whether they were online guides, picture applications, or even books like this one. Think about how your photography has evolved from simple snapshots to more composed and artistic photographs.

3. Overcoming Obstacles: Whether it's getting the hang of manual settings, handling challenging lighting, or just coming up with ideas, every photographer has obstacles to overcome. Think back on the challenges you faced and the means by which you overcome them. These events play a critical role in molding your development and fortitude as a photographer.

4. Distinctive Style and Expression: Whether it's a penchant for vivid hues, simple compositions, or unposed photos, you've gradually established a distinctive style. Your creative voice is now an extension of your iPhone. Consider how your photographic style has changed and how your images now showcase your own viewpoint.

5. Memorable Moments: Recall some of your most treasured pictures and the narratives that accompanied them. What was it about those times that was unique? How did you record them using your iPhone so that you and others could relate to them?

6. Technological Developments: The camera technology in the iPhone has advanced, bringing additional features and functionalities. Consider the ways in which these developments have affected your photography. Think about how each update has affected your work, from enhanced low-light performance to sophisticated editing capabilities.

[187]

7. Community and Feedback: It may be really beneficial to interact with other photographers and get their input. Think back on the groups you've joined, the criticism you've encountered, and the resources for assistance you've discovered. What impact has this encounter had on the way you shoot photos?

8. Prospective Goals: Consider your future goals for your iPhone photography while you reflect on the past. Do you have any new methods, genres, or projects you'd want to try? You are on a continuous journey where every obstacle is a chance for improvement.

REMEMBERING FUTURE FEATURES AND UPDATES

making the most of your gadgets and apps in the ever changing world of technology requires keeping up with upcoming upgrades and improvements. Here are several ways to stay up to date with the newest advancements in the tech world, whether you're a tech enthusiast, a professional in the area, or simply someone who wants to get the most out of their gadgets:

1. Refer to authorized sources: Keeping up with official announcements from software developers or device makers is the most dependable strategy to keep current. This entails keeping a watch on official Apple events like WWDC (Worldwide Developers Conference), developer blogs, and the Apple Newsroom for information on Apple products. You may be sure you're getting reliable information straight from the source

by subscribing to these publications'
newsletters and alerts.

2. Join Tech Communities: Participating in
forums and communities related to
technology might provide first access to new
features and upgrades. Discussions and leaks
on sites like Reddit, Stack Exchange, and
niche tech communities might offer you an
idea of what's to come. Just keep in mind to
confirm any information you discover with
reputable sources.

3. Subscribe to Tech News Outlets: A lot of
YouTube channels and websites devoted to
tech news provide updates on the newest
innovations and developments in the field.
News and commentary on new versions are
often covered by publications and channels
like MKBHD or Linus Tech Tips, as well as
outlets like TechCrunch, The Verge, and
CNET.

4. Take Part in Beta Programs: A lot of IT
businesses let customers test new features
before they are made public via beta

programs. By taking part in these programs, you may help shape the final version by providing input and get early access to new functionality.

Examine the Release Notes: Developers often provide release notes with updates that include all of the new features, enhancements, and problem fixes. You may get a thorough understanding of the changes and how they may affect your usage of the technology by reading these notes.

6. Make Use of Social Media: Keeping up with news from IT businesses and industry insiders may be achieved by using social media platforms. You may keep informed by following influencers, tech journalists, and official corporate accounts.

7. Attend Industry Events: Webinars, conferences, and seminars may provide in-depth knowledge on future trends and technology. These gatherings provide a forum for conversation on the direction of technology and often include speeches by

prominent figures in the field.

8. Examine Developer Resources: If you're interested in going further, you may learn more about forthcoming features by looking through developer documentation and resources. This is especially helpful for comprehending modifications to application programming interfaces (APIs) and software development kits (SDKs).

ENCOURAGEMENT TO KEEP PRACTICING AND INNOVATING

Whether it's technology, photography, or any other endeavor, learning a new talent or art always involves obstacles and periods of uncertainty. When things don't appear to be moving forward or when there are challenges, it's simple to become discouraged. Nonetheless, it's important to keep in mind that perseverance and creativity are the keys to success.

Accept the Process

Every master started out as a novice, and every accomplishment comes from long hours of hard work and devotion. Both the goal and the journey have significance. Accept every step—no matter how small—and understand that every setback is a chance for improvement. The secret is to never stop honing your craft, expanding your horizons, and practicing.

Innovate with Passion: Creativity and

exploration are the foundations of an atmosphere where innovation flourishes. Don't be scared to try out novel methods, resources, or concepts. Most of the time, breakthroughs come from trying new things. Your own viewpoint is a great advantage, and you open the door for new and fascinating discoveries by continuing to be inquisitive and receptive.

Honor advancements

No matter how little the steps you've taken to get there, take the time to recognize and enjoy them. Every accomplishment, no matter how great or little, is evidence of your diligence and hard effort. Honoring these successes may inspire drive and a feeling of achievement that spurs on further work.

Seek Motivation and Input

Keep yourself surrounded by inspirational people and don't be afraid to ask for advice from others. Joining a group of people who share your interests may open your eyes, promote personal development, and give you the encouragement you need to get through difficult situations. Giving yourself constructive criticism may help you improve your abilities and generate original ideas.

Remain Resilient

In every artistic or technological activity, resilience is essential. Even though there may be obstacles and frustrating times, keeping a positive outlook and pushing through challenges can eventually result in advancement. Always keep in mind that every obstacle presents an opportunity to improve your abilities and get a better comprehension of your field.

Keep learning

Since the world is always changing, so too should your skill set. Keep abreast on the newest methods, trends, and technology. Not only does lifelong learning keep your skills current, but it also feeds your creativity and enthusiasm.

Made in the USA
Monee, IL
23 December 2024

75238399R00108